THE UNVEILING

An American Teacher in a Saudi Palace
by

Kristin Decker

The Unveiling is based upon a true story. Names, characters, chronology and some events have been altered to protect the privacy and innocence of those who worked for the family and those remaining in Saudi Arabia.

"The Unveiling" by Kristin Decker. ISBN 1-58939-912-9; 1-58939-911-0 (casebound).

Manufactured in the United States of America.

Dedication:

To my husband, Randal, for his steadfast love and support.
To Aslan and Cheyenne for loving Randal and me.

TABLE OF CONTENTS

1. *Halas!* Finished! 1

2. Providence 11

3. Women in Black 29

4. Politics in Paradise 40

5. "We Are Muslim" 53

6. A Path to Success 64

7. *Bedouin* Beauty 77

8. Forbidden! 87

9. Into the Valleys 100

10. The Wrong Side of the Fence 108

11. Searched 118

12. Revenge Takes a Pawn 124

13. Shifting Sands 132

14. Leaving Kansas 140

15. *"Dhimmi"* 152

16. Free 160

Epilogue 169

Glossary 185

Endnotes 187

Bibliography 189

1.

HALAS! FINISHED!

THE LOW HUM of an engine announced the arrival of the moving van as it parked in front of my villa in Saudi Arabia. I pulled back the heavy brocade drapes along the front window and peered into the dark Arabian skies. Under the dim light of a towering street lamp, I could make out the silhouettes of several men in long robes as they piled out of the van and slammed the doors shut. They'd been sent to pack my belongings and ship them back to America because my husband and I were suddenly being expelled from the country.

I kept hoping that God would intervene on our behalf, so we could continue tutoring the children of a powerful Arabian prince and princess. Unfortunately, every resource our Western upbringing had taught us to utilize for solving problems was proving unreliable. We thought that if our relationships with the prince and princess were based on mutual respect, we could resolve conflicts, but they turned on us instantly without evidence. We believed that if we worked hard we would be valued, but credit for our work was given to another. We thought that believing in Their Highnesses' dreams and showing we cared would foster good will, but the princess blamed us for ruining her dreams. We didn't understand why our good intentions had failed. If God didn't act soon, all of our dreams would be lost.

Fighting the tears in my eyes, I put the dogs in the kitchen and watched Randy dial another phone number. "Can't you reach Prince Faisal?" I asked, thinking the prince would be reasonable.

"I've tried." He turned toward me.

I saw a fear in his eyes I had never seen before. "What is it?"

He took a deep breath. "Kris, the prince's secretary won't put my calls through and now . . . They're threatening us with jail."

"Jail! For what?" I asked, wondering how discussions disintegrated so quickly to threats.

"I don't know, but if we demand our rights, the secretary says we'll have to wait in a Saudi jail if we want a hearing with the prince of Riyadh. Do you know what they'd do to us in a Saudi jail?"

Though I'd always tried to push the stories out of my mind, I knew exactly what they could do; floggings, torture, and even rape. My stomach churned as I shut the dogs in the kitchen.

There was a light rap on our front door. Randy swung it open and looked into the troubled eyes of a dear friend. Akbar, a palace servant, had been to our villa earlier that day to confiscate the car we'd driven to and from the palace school. He bowed with respect but hesitated to enter. When Randy assured him it wasn't his fault, Akbar entered slowly. Several men followed him carrying boxes and crates.

I couldn't hold back the tears any longer and ran out onto the porch. Sitting on the marble steps, I tried to push back the sobs caught in my throat. I looked back toward Randy, needing him to comfort me, but he was consumed with trying to stop the nightmare. As I looked across the compound wall toward the glimmering night-lights of Riyadh, I felt overwhelming grief and loss. When would God's deliverance come?

One of the packers paused before going back inside. I had seen him at the palace, but he spoke no English. Our greetings had always been limited to polite nods. He looked at me with compassion, and then with his hands, he made the shape of a heart across his chest, opened his palms toward me and bowed his head. He was telling me how sorry he was this was happening to us. His act of kindness crossed all boundaries and though I wanted to reach out and grasp his hands in friendship, it was strictly forbidden for a woman to touch a Muslim man. I managed a warm smile and whispered my thanks in Arabic, "Shukrhan." He walked somberly into the villa.

I started back inside when I heard a car coming down the street. Our neighbors, Mohammed and Anna, pulled into their driveway. As they got out, Mohammed glanced toward our villa. Anna cast an alarmed gaze my way. They slammed their car doors shut and rushed toward me.

"Kristin! What's happening?" yelled Anna as she pulled off her black scarf and cape.

"We're being expelled from the kingdom!"

"When?" she asked running toward me.

"Tonight!"

She threw her arms around me and I held her tightly as the chaos swirled around me. The movers walked past us carrying boxes and shouting orders. Mohammed, now by Randy's side, anxiously tried to help him call influential people. Randy dialed number after number, ending each call with a frustrated slamming of the receiver.

Suddenly the dogs bounded down the walk and whimpered at my feet. They seemed to know something was terribly wrong. When I knelt to comfort them, they licked my face with their wet and sticky tongues. I wrapped my arms around their necks and a devastating realization crossed my mind. We didn't have any veterinarian certificates for them to travel. We had been so sure we could work out an understanding, we hadn't thought about the dogs' papers.

It was late, and I knew that all the vets were closed. For a heartrending moment, I imagined my precious pets frightened and helpless among the other abandoned dogs that stalked and ravaged the ruddy sand dunes throughout the desert. I shivered with panic and clung to their beautiful golden coats, wondering how anyone could think so little of animals.

I looked up. "Anna, how will we get them out of the country? We don't have their papers!"

"We'll think of something," she said, but I could hear the worry in her voice.

When Akbar walked by, she grabbed his sleeve. "Can you help us with the dogs? They need traveling papers."

He looked at the dogs through teary eyes. Fortunately, he knew a doctor and agreed to take them to his house. Like innocent children, Aslan and Cheyenne looked at me dependently with their tender brown eyes. Akbar patted their soft heads and took them by their leashes.

"I hope this tragedy won't overshadow that these servants love you and Randy," said Anna.

I nodded, realizing how the servants had responded so thoughtfully to us throughout our stay in Riyadh. Looking back, I saw the kind-hearted servant packing three brass camels that I had recently purchased at a bazaar. I held up my hand for him to stop. I wanted Anna to have them. She protested, but I motioned to the servant to bring me the camels. I placed them in her hands. Reluctantly, she accepted them and then suggested we go to her villa for some tea.

Trying to ignore the yells of the packers, we headed toward her villa and rested in her neat and orderly home. Her smile made me feel almost normal again. The tea felt good on my throat. I don't remember much of what we talked about; something about the upcoming ball at the embassy, the bazaar at the expatriates' center...any topic other than what was happening to us.

When the packing was finished and I had regained some composure, we returned to my villa. On the porch, Akbar was saying

3

good-bye to my husband. When he broke into tears, Randy put his arm around him. The two men stood still as our dear friend wept on my husband's shoulder. At last Akbar muttered something, got in the van and headed toward the palace. He'd return within the hour to drive us to the airport. If he didn't return with my dogs and their papers, I feared I'd never see them again.

Mohammed and Anna stood with us in the middle of our living room. Except for the furniture that belonged to the compound, our villa was empty. The fresh flowers were gone as well as the Monet prints, the china and the classics that lined the bookcase. My small knick-knacks, embroidered quilt and Oriental rugs were packed away in a box in the back of the moving van. My home had been stripped of the symbols of civilization that often veiled the shortcomings and frailties of man's inhumanity to man and what it was like to be alone or forgotten. Perhaps a preoccupation with them also numbed my senses to what was most important and prevented me from making the necessary connections for living authentically in the world.

It had been our choice to immerse ourselves in a culture so vastly different from our Western culture, but we believed that was the best way to learn about another way of life. We were certain it would be far more profitable than merely reading a book or earning a degree. And while we respected the historical accomplishments of Islamic culture in math, science and medicine, Saudi Arabia was a culture dominated by Wahabbi clerical teachings that dismissed the faculty of human reasoning and focused on rote memorization of the *Qur'an*. Saudi Arabia was a culture without exposure to Aristotle or Plato, Aquinas or Anselm and the ensuing philosophical debates. It was a culture without a Renaissance, a Reformation, Enlightenment, a Magna Carta, Constitution or Bill of Rights. But I was also wondering if the West had elevated reason so much, that a certain level of spiritual illiteracy had developed and crippled our efforts to understand the Middle East. How well could we relate to this fundamental culture with its legalistic approach to God and life?

Looking around, I noticed the dog fur that lined the corners of the room and the dust from the nearby sand dunes that had already settled upon the tables and chairs. I apologized to Anna for the unsightly dirt and dust. It was a last attempt at owning something that was no longer mine.

Mohammed sat on a sofa and looked sadly around. "How did this happen, Randy?"

"We don't really know, but we were grilled about proselytizing Muslims. An acquaintance brought our personal Bible through customs. He distracted the guards by pointing to our videos. It was for our personal use. We'd never proselytize anyone because it means immediate expulsion."

"And supposedly we insulted the royal family," I said, "but we admire them."

"You spoke more highly of them than some of their subjects," Mohammed said with a hint of sarcasm. "But insulting them is a deportable offense."

"We worked hard to show respect for the Islamic way of life. To me it was insulting not to be allowed to drive, to never go anywhere without my husband and to always wear *that!*" I pointed toward the black cloak and scarf every woman was forced to wear in public. "But I did it out of *respect!*" I walked toward the *abaya* and veil and picked them up. Wearing them had labeled me as a second-class citizen. I strode through the sliding glass door to the dumpster. Hoping never to feel the humiliation of draping them over my shoulders and hair again, I shredded the veil from top to bottom and threw both onto the pile of trash. After I shred the veil, I recalled a verse in the Gospel of Matthew that described how the veil in the Holy Temple in Jerusalem was used to separate the Holy of Holies from the altar. When Christ died on the cross, the veil ripped open wide from top to bottom.

"And there are more accusations," Randy continued. He explained that a few months before a woman we worked with took a vacation in Europe but never returned to Saudi. The FBI questioned her about some kind of terrorist threat. The agents even called the princess about her. Though rumors circulated the palace that she had associated with terrorists, we never believed the accusations. Recalling what a palace insider had secretly leaked to me, I related how the princess began suspecting that we were involved with terrorism too.

Randy's eyes reddened as he said, "And after we cared so much for them."

"Do you know which terrorist organization?" asked Mohammed.

"There was some kind of link to Osama Bin Laden," said Randy. "Our friend dated an American pilot who reported seeing one of Bin Laden's followers in Paris, but the report was turned against the American. I guess his Palestinian co-pilot had even tried to crash the plane with a powerful Saudi dignitary onboard. I don't understand the details, but it sounds like a mess."

Mohammed's jaw dropped and his face paled. "Bin Laden! He lives and breathes to see the Saudi royal family destroyed. What's your friend doing with him?"

Anna shook her head at Mohammed, but the damage was done,

and my heart raced. "She's not!" I blurted. "The Palestinian co-pilot turned the American pilot's report against him, probably to protect himself from the authorities."

Because of the ensuing fear, all of our attempts at communication had been scorned. No one had investigated the facts or considered two sides of a story. But to us, the charges didn't make any sense. How could we be working with terrorists *and* proselytizing Muslims?

"I guess we were prideful to think we could resolve everything diplomatically," I said.

"Don't be too hard on yourselves," said Mohammed. "This happens in business circles all the time. I'm sorry it happened to you. I just hope you get your severance pay."

I looked away, not wanting Randy to see my worry. Though we had been promised three months pay, we'd only received two weeks. We had enough money to make one more mortgage payment. What if we lost our home in California as well?

Randy said, "Maybe I should go ahead and sit in jail and wait to clear my name before Prince Salman . . . you know, the governor in charge of local disputes."

I gasped; every muscle in my body tightened. Jail was a dangerous place for an American Christian. And if we spoke with Prince Salman, he'd learn that the prince who hired us had defied him by opening a private school over his stern objections. Prince Faisal would be dishonored. However, if we didn't speak with Prince Salman, the school would be ruined and our lives disrupted.

"Jail!" exclaimed Mohammed.

"The secretary threatened me with jail if I didn't cooperate by turning over my papers," Randy said angrily.

"You don't ever want to end up in a Saudi jail," warned Mohammed. "Listen to me, when the guards find out what you're accused of, you'll regret it. Fatalism lets people believe you deserve the evil that's come your way. No one will intervene on your behalf."

Randy was silent. I knew what justice meant to him, so I pleaded with him to fight the battle on familiar ground some other day. Mohammed grabbed Randy by the shoulder and told him how justice was executed in Saudi. He knew of a courtier who was thrown into jail, tortured mercilessly and then beheaded for not carrying out a prince's command. The poor man didn't even know what he had been accused of.

Randy studied Mohammed's face intently. Finally, he relented and agreed not to risk jail, for my sake.

Seid, an East Indian we had befriended, entered through the open door. He had frequently explained to us how people from Pakistan, India and the Philippines experienced horrible tragedies in Saudi Arabia. Though their lives could be in danger, embassies from developing countries felt powerless to intervene. The stories Seid told were so outrageous that it was hard to believe them. I couldn't imagine such evil existing on the earth, and I didn't want to wrongly accuse someone or some institution of a crime. But after what had happened to us, we began to believe Seid. He was also convinced that because we were Americans, people would listen to us tell their stories. But who else would take the tales of tragedy seriously?

Seid said, "Sir, you must fight for us! God will show you what to do." Randy looked at him with compassion, saying he'd do whatever he could.

Once again I heard the moving van as it pulled into my driveway. Akbar entered and handed me the dogs' traveling papers. I was so grateful that I reached out to embrace him. Embarrassed by my emotional display, he moved out of my grasp and stood beside Randy. Akbar had worked a near miracle, and I didn't know how to thank him appropriately.

Akbar addressed Randy. "Sir, the secretary say you make threat to call out Marines on them."

"The Marines! A civilian can't call out the damned Marines," fumed Randy. "I told the secretary that the embassy was closed so a Marine guard answered the phone when I called."

"And the secretary tell Prince Faisal you curse his family," continued Akbar.

I closed my eyes and fought my anger and hot tears. I felt utterly betrayed for I would never curse the royal family.

Akbar addressed Randy. "Sir, your plane leave soon."

Randy looked sadly toward me. "Well, I guess it's a plane ticket home or prison. No one is interested in listening to us."

Akbar hauled our suitcases to the van. Randy and I followed him outside. If Randy and I lost everything else, we had each other and our integrity. These were the only things that mattered anymore. Aslan and Cheyenne were still in their crates and whimpered when they saw me. As we drove down the street, I looked sadly through the windows of the home we had made in Saudi Arabia. The street lamps cast shadows among its desolate rooms. The place was silent, waiting for a new American family. I wanted to warn them, whoever they would be.

While Akbar drove quietly along the dimly lit freeway, Anna said to me, "In my devotions this morning I came across the verse, *Blessed are the persecuted, for theirs is the Kingdom of Heaven.* I think it's for you and Randy."

I couldn't imagine how our losses could be a blessing, but I did know that God required his followers to pray for those who persecuted them and to even pray for blessings to come upon them.

When we arrived at the terminal and headed toward the check-in counter, we passed a long line of Indian women just entering the country. They were draped in colorful silk saris with their jet-black hair flowing bountifully under an array of clips and scarves. When I saw their sponsor, donned in a white robe and head scarf, barking orders at them, fear for them welled up within me. With Seid's reminder fresh in my mind, I wondered which of the women might have been promised jobs caring for children or cleaning magnificent homes, when in fact they would end up being held as slaves, assaulted sexually or abandoned and left to beg on the streets. I longed to tell them to go back to India before it was too late. Sensing my emotions, Randy grabbed my hand and pulled me along. I whispered a fervent prayer for their welfare.

Mohammed, Akbar and Randy checked our dogs and luggage in at the counter, and then we headed for the customs gate.

Akbar placed his hand on Randy's shoulder. "Sir, no one blame you for revenge."

"Justice will come another day, Akbar."

"If this my country, I go after this person. I kill them," whispered Akbar.

Alarmed, Randy shook his head sternly. "No, no, my friend. Not revenge."

Akbar sighed and relented. "Okay, sir. No revenge."

Mohammed peered into my carry-on luggage and froze. I followed his gaze to my Bible that lay exposed on top. It was an illegal item, so Anna leaned down and pulled another book over it.

The guard motioned for us to pass through the check and shouted, "*Halas!*"

"*Halas*, finished," I repeated sadly. The words, *It is finished,* drifted through my mind, reminding me of God's forgiveness and the place that suffering had in a believer's life. I felt as if I were traveling through the valley of the shadow of death. But, I wondered, could forgiveness really soothe my anger and heal my wounds? If forgiveness were a path toward healing, God would have to help me follow him down that path by sending his spirit and power.

Anna embraced me. "Write us. We want to know what happens to you."

"I will." I watched Randy press some cash into Akbar's hand for all he'd done, but Akbar refused to take it. Fighting his humiliation, Randy put it in his pocket. We showed our boarding passes to the guard. Randy placed his Swiss army knife and keys on the counter. The guard picked up the knife and tossed it into a wooden box littered with other forbidden items. Randy picked up his keys and walked through the gate. We turned and waved good-bye to our dear friends. They waved back somberly. They were Muslim and Christian, black, white and brown, and sadness drained all color and barriers from their faces.

Randy and I walked alone toward the gate and sat in the stiff plastic chairs. I shivered in the cold night air and pulled my coat collar closer. The glare of overhead lighting made me blink at the blurry figures looming overhead. Two men were ogling and mocking me from behind the railing of a second story terrace. No longer covered with the black robe, they considered me provocative. Though I wondered if they would ever learn self-control, I found their rudeness negligible in comparison with the brokenness of my heart. I turned away from the immature men and grieved over the careless act of abandon the prince and princess had allowed.

Our flight was finally announced. I held onto Randy's arm and trudged down the ramp toward the plane. Randy turned restlessly in the airline seat beside me. Sleep eluded us even though it was now 3:00 a.m. Since the FBI had harassed our friend, we were afraid to return to the United States.

"What if something was planted in our luggage?" I worried aloud.

"I hadn't thought of that." Randy looked down at our tickets. "You know, we have a stopover in Greece. We should get off in Athens and disappear for a while."

"You mean . . ." I could hardly get the words out. "Be on the run, like fugitives?"

"We are fugitives. We're being thrown out of Saudi Arabia because we're terrorists."

"Don't ever say that!" I scolded. "We are *not*!"

"Of course not. But according to someone in the Saudi government, we are anti-Islamic and dangerous. For now, there's no safe place for us."

"Then we need to hide out while we sort this through."

We were both quiet. "The children," he said slowly. "I never had a chance to say good-bye to them. That's what hurts me the most. Leaving the children like this."

He slumped into the seat and I closed my eyes, wishing I could tell the young prince and princess how much we cared about them and their futures.

9

I gazed out the dark window. What had gone wrong? How had Randy and I ended up terrified, unemployed and homeless? We'd entrusted our lives and our dreams to the Saudi royal family. How could they betray our trust? I believed that God in his providence had guided us to Saudi Arabia. Why did he allow us to experience this painful loss? Did he have a greater purpose?

I longed to expunge every thought of Saudi Arabia from my heart, but to do so meant to shut out part of myself. My life was now inextricably intertwined with the Islamic state, and I would have to accept that and find meaning in it.

A tiredness I'd never felt before overwhelmed me. I wrapped a blanket around me as the plane rumbled toward take off and its stop in the birthplace of Western civilization, Athens. Perhaps in Greece I could reflect upon the cultural differences and limitations of my Western worldview that prevented me from understanding the confusing circumstances I'd just experienced. I thought back to where Randy and I were several years before, trying to find the answers to the unrelenting questions that challenged my faith. Perhaps, my questions would strengthen it.

2.

PROVIDENCE

MYSTICAL AND FARAWAY places had cast alluring spells over me from my youth. In daydreams and fantasies, I explored the Great Wall of China, touched gilded icons in a Greek Orthodox Church and climbed to the top of Big Ben. I rode camels across sand dunes and watched sunsets from the capstones of pyramids. Where others shivered at the thought of bitter cold winters in northern lands, I saw palaces of glittering ice nestled in soft blankets of snow. Where others saw only blistering, barren deserts, I had visions of shimmering mirages arising from golden sands. No matter where I went, I knew that every spring would bring pink cherry blossoms in China and purple irises in the deserts of Arabia. The beauty of God's creation would be enough cause to forgive any winter its harshness or any summer its searing heat.

In 1995, these dreams, and the stress of living in the Los Angeles area, led me to convince my husband Randy to consider teaching overseas. My brother and his wife had lived and taught overseas – three years in Saudi Arabia, three in Moscow and two in South Africa. During our summer get-togethers, they brought exotic gifts from their travels. I loved the Russian eggs, the Bahraini pottery, and the weavings from Nepal, but Randy thought they made our house look like a museum. He just didn't have the heart of an adventurer.

While Randy tolerated his job as an elementary teacher, it was a career he had never planned upon. A sincere Christian, he attended an ecumenical seminary after college. We met and married during our seminary years and after graduating assumed we'd find a position within a church setting. Our theological beliefs were a moderate mixture of liberal and conservative, and unfortunately, every denomination we tried to affiliate with seemed an uncomfortable fit. The decision to teach was disparaging for Randy, but I believed God had a greater purpose.

Randy coped by developing a love for his life away from work. Day trips throughout the Southwest in his old Porsche, workouts on his home gym in a corner of the patio, dinners and movies out with me; these were all reasons to stay. I knew he had reasons to go too. We had the Volvo, the Porsche and the townhome in Pasadena. We also had the debt to go along with them. We kept current, but Randy talked more and more of his teaching career with Los Angeles Unified Schools as, "The Golden Handcuffs." He felt trapped and questioned God's purpose in his teaching career.

While attending university in Canada, I decided to become a teacher. My many teachers had instilled in me a love for learning, especially my high school English and history teachers. Perhaps because I grew up in small rural towns and wanted to see the world, I had decided it was a magical and awe-inspiring place. I hoped to empower and equip young people to discover its many wonders as well. Regardless of the low esteem our contemporary culture seemed to express toward education, I thought teaching was a noble career. For me, teaching a child to read and think was one of the more important social contributions that could be made.

One evening after dinner, Randy and I talked seriously about the direction our lives were taking. Randy stretched out on the sofa and I sat across from him. Cheyenne and Aslan, our beautiful golden retrievers, curled up calmly at our feet.

"My brother paid off his mortgage with the money he made in Saudi Arabia," I said.

Randy tilted his head. "But Jack lived in Palmdale. He owed half what we owe."

"Still," I persisted, "their school paid a good salary, provided housing and transportation, benefits, round-trip air travel home once a year – and it was all tax exempt."

"Housing and transportation? What'd they give them? A tent and a camel?"

"Oh, please." He knew how to annoy me. My brother, Jack, and his wife, Tyan, enjoyed their time in Saudi. It surprised me really. Tyan was quite the feminist, and the *Sharia* law, or religious law, governed every aspect of Arabian life. I had trouble picturing Tyan on the streets of Riyadh draped in the mandatory black covering known as the *abaya*. She couldn't drive either, but she said that the financial security made personal sacrifices worthwhile.

Randy paused briefly. "How much did they make again?"

"About $100,000 a year. They paid off their house and built up their retirement."

"There are job fairs in the U.S. for overseas teaching jobs, right?"

"There's one every year in Monterey," I said, praying silently that God would give Randy a willing heart to attend.

"Well, let's go . . . just to see what God might open up. But, no promises!" he said.

Trying not to look too excited, I promised to call Jack and get information on the next fair.

We decided to keep the matter in prayer and see how events unfolded, and by the end of the month, Randy and I were driving up the winding coastal highway of California. The beautiful Monterey inn lay nestled among the tall pines at the foot of coastal mountains. Its red tile roof crowned white stucco walls and mission-style archways. Towering palms lined the long driveway and lazy bougainvilleas fell over walls and arbors. Geraniums, petunias and pansies splashed a rainbow of yellow, pink and blue along windowsills and doorways from a variety of Mexican clay pots. The ocean lay just the other side of the freeway granting the breeze its desire to blow inland.

"Nice place for a job fair," I said as Randy wheeled his 1984 Porsche Targa into the lane.

"Overseas principals just want to blow their expense accounts on a California vacation."

I looked at him and broke into a half smile. "You're such a cynic."

We settled into our room and wandered through the fragrant gardens, looking for a private place where we could pray together and ask God for his guidance. We found a wooden bench and prayed for God to lead us as a good shepherd leads his flock. We decided that we would only accept a position if we were in agreement about it. If one of us objected to an assignment, we'd assume it wasn't meant for us.

We then followed a sign reading *Overseas Educators,* to a lounge where notebooks listing all the participating schools were arranged. Each entry listed a description of the school, the openings for the coming year and the financial packages. Shanghai, Malaysia, Budapest, Bahrain— I couldn't believe it! The book listed all the places I had dreamed about visiting.

Randy flipped through the listings. "Hey, here's a school in Saudi Arabia with two students."

"Oh, sure!" I said, skimming the information for a school in Shanghai.

He read the details for me. 'A teaching couple with credentials in multiple subjects is needed to provide a core education for two students. The teachers will lead a team of seven other teachers who provide instruction in a variety of subjects. It pays $36,000 a year each, plus health insurance, housing in a private villa, a new car and round-trip air transportation.'

I figured it must be a mistake and looked for the page on Beijing. When Randy realized that the school where Tyan and Jack worked paid better, we decided to interview with that school instead of the two-student school.

As the evening wore on, the inn buzzed with lively conversation, and job fair participants continued to arrive. A crackling fire warmed the lobby where Randy and I went to get acquainted with other teachers who also yearned to travel and live abroad. I caught a glimpse of a professional-looking gentleman in a navy blue suit. He brushed the fabric arrogantly as if he knew how much better dressed he was than everyone else. He had a fair complexion with hazel eyes, and thinning auburn hair. For a brief moment, our eyes met, and I shuddered inexplicably. I quickly looked away, wondering what I had sensed.

Once the teaching candidates were settled in the large conference room, the director of the conference rose to the podium and welcomed everyone. After the usual formalities, he took the time to comment on particular schools represented. My mind wandered until he mentioned the two-student school in Riyadh. It was a private tutorial position with a wealthy family. The position had a compensation package competitive with American schools in the region, but it only involved teaching four hours a day. He encouraged couples interested in banking extra money to give the school some thought. Randy and I agreed to look at the position again.

Near the front, a young woman spoke in a sharp tone. "You said they want a teaching couple. I'm single and think that's discriminatory."

Randy looked at me and rolled his eyes; I ignored him.

The director responded, "I know this is California, but you have to understand these are international schools. Laws of equal opportunity do not bind them. It's to their financial advantage to house married couples. A lot of schools take singles, but some countries aren't the best place for single women. For instance, Saudi Arabia doesn't allow women many personal liberties at all. You'd have to cover and wouldn't be allowed to drive. Since men and women are not allowed to commingle, dating is illegal. Frankly, I don't know why a single woman would want to go some place like that."

Randy wondered if I could handle the religious restrictions, but I shrugged my shoulders knowing it would only be for a couple of years. In spite of our good resumes, I couldn't imagine such a prestigious family would consider us anyway.

The next day we interviewed with four schools– three in Saudi Arabia, including the two-student tutorial, and one in Shanghai, China. The interviewer for the small Saudi school was the nicely dressed businessman I'd noticed the day before who had made me shudder. He introduced himself as Abdullah Al-Rasheed, but in the interview, he was actually charming, polite and approachable. I regretted prejudging him.

I was completely surprised when he said we were his first choice and that if we accepted the position we would be working for a prominent prince. The prince's distinguished lineage ranked him among the more powerful princes, meaning that he could become king one day. Mr. Al-Rasheed added, "I represent His Highness and he relies on me to take care of his business. He will accept whoever I recommend." Then he addressed me. "Even American women must wear the *abaya*, the black cloak that covers the whole body. How do you feel about that?"

Though covering was a sign of oppression to me, I also considered an opportunity to work with future leaders worth a personal sacrifice. "I believe it would be worth it," I said.

Mr. Al-Rasheed smiled and then looked at us intently. "One last thing, what religion do you observe?"

"We are Christians," I said.

"Perhaps you noticed our resumes include theological studies," Randy added.

"Yes, I did, but there are no Christian churches in Saudi Arabia, so please, do not bring your Bibles or wear a cross."

The request surprised me because it had been my understanding that Christians were considered, 'People of the book,' by Muslims. Though disappointed, Randy and I agreed to keep the terms.

Mr. Al-Rasheed told us about the children. They were very bright. The young princess, Samira, read constantly and was a delight to teach. The young prince, Majid, was enthusiastic about science. He needed a lot of coaxing to finish his work, so we'd have to be creative to keep his attention. With only one child at a time, we were sure we could keep him focused.

Mr. Al-Rasheed related that the school had been closed early in 1994 due to political issues, but made it clear that the prince took exceptionally good care of the teachers. The princess was most excited about the school opening. She believed that if her children attended the best Western universities, they would be able to converse with leaders from around the world and help lead Saudi Arabia into the future. She wanted them to receive a good education and keep their Islamic faith.

Her vision for her children was an inspiration, and I wanted to support it however I could.

We had several offers from school directors, and though we were flattered to have a choice, we were in a quandary as what to do and wanted to discuss the matter and pray together for God's direction. We asked Mr. Al-Rasheed if we could get back to him with our decision.

We quickly ruled out the offer in Jeddah because the pay was so low it wouldn't be worth our while. As for Shanghai, it paid substantially more than the prince paid, but if Randy and I accepted the private tutorial in Saudi, we might have an opportunity to help bring about good in a troubled region of the world. We wondered if God might not be opening the door for us, but we also wondered how secure the position was. We decided to corner the director of Overseas Educators and see if we could get a more experienced perspective. We found him in the lobby, and he invited us to sit with him and talk over our concerns.

He was silent for a moment. "Like I said at the beginning, it's a great opportunity. But what concerns me is that I don't think the applicants understand how unique the situation is. This isn't an ordinary international school run by Americans for the expatriate community. This is a private school run by a prince. You'll be working at a palace. Who knows what that would be like? Will there be armed guards in the room with you? Will you be free with teaching content? Will you have direct access to the parents, or will everything have to go through palace courtiers? And if you have to go through courtiers, how do you know the prince and princess will get an accurate portrayal of the facts? Who knows what kind of palace intrigue goes on over there? This could be an experience right out of the Arabian Nights."

I shuddered. "You're scaring me."

"I don't mean to do that, but you're new to international teaching. You have to weigh the risks of each position. For instance, in Shanghai, you'd be working in a Communist country."

"Los Angeles schools have students from around the world and nearly a hundred different languages are spoken. We've been surrounded by different cultures for years," I explained.

"But in Shanghai, we'd be working in an American run school," Randy pointed out.

"Exactly," the director said. "If you want the security of working for Americans in an American school, go with Shanghai. But if you're looking for a once in a lifetime experience, go with the prince. Either way, you must weigh both risk and reward. The real question is, how much adventure do you want?" He stood and shook our hands. "Let me know what you decide."

After he left I said, "We've taught cross-culturally for so long, I'm not going to worry. Besides, I feel mystically drawn to the Saudi children. I can't get them out of my mind even though I've always wanted to teach in China. What do you want to do?"

"I admire this prince and his family's vision. I've always wondered why I ended up teaching after graduating from seminary. Maybe teaching a prince was part of God's plan." He paused for a moment before he smiled and said, "Let's have an adventure!"

The following day we met Abdullah Al-Rasheed in the restaurant and conducted our business over coffee. Randy and I eagerly signed the prince's contract. I was impressed by the stately letterhead and was relieved to see in writing that potential conflicts would be settled amicably. It convinced me that signing on with the prince was the right decision. Mr. Al-Rasheed promised to keep in touch and help us with the visa process.

As soon as we returned to our home in southern California, we searched bookstores everywhere to find any information we could about life inside the mysterious Kingdom of Saudi Arabia. There were hardly any books on the shelves, so we read *Not Without my Daughter,* by Betty Mahmoody, and then *Lawrence of Arabia*. We finally found a couple written by people who had lived and worked in Saudi and read them from cover to cover. We wanted to know everything about the country and people we were going to work for.

In 1745, the founder of modern day Saudi Arabia, Sheik Muhammad Saud, lived in a small *wadi* town, *Diriyah*, north of the modern capital city of Riyadh. At *Diriyah* he joined forces with a fundamentalist teacher, Muhammad Al-Wahhab, who had reformed the practices of Islam so they would be consistent with the ascetic teachings of a tenth century teacher, Mohammed Al-Hanbal. Together, Al-Saud and Al-Wahhab were a formidable force, bringing their reformed brand of Islam to all neighboring tribes often at the point of the sword. The Al-Saud raided the rival ruling clan of the Al-Rasheeds, forcing the Rasheed family north into Kuwait and Bahrain. In the late 1800s, the Rasheeds returned and ran the Saud clan out of Riyadh. A young descendant of Muhammad Saud, Abdul Aziz, fled shamefully on a camel with his father to Kuwait. *

By 1901, Abdul Aziz had grown into a tall, stocky and determined young man. He planned to restore his family's honor and returned to Riyadh. In the middle of the night, he scaled the walls of a brick fortress named *Mismaak* and took the life of the Al-Rasheed governor while he slept. Abdul Aziz threw the governor's head into the city streets below and proudly reestablished his family's rule in the region. Unlike the sheiks before him, he wanted to unify the warring tribes of Arabia. After conquering Mecca, Medina, and numerous Arab tribes, he declared himself king in 1932. He built alliances with remaining *Bedouin* tribes, primarily through marriage. He established a connection with the tribal leaders through the *majlis,* a meeting where the common man could speak with the king face to face and bring him their needs and concerns. He considered this practice a type of desert democracy since his people had a voice.

During the 1940s, Abdul Aziz met with the U.S. president, Franklin D. Roosevelt. The two leaders established an alliance that has lasted through to modern times. Saudi Arabia promised to supply the U.S. with oil, and in return, the U.S. promised to provide protection for the fledgling country from its hostile neighbors. When FDR asked Aziz for his opinion on establishing a state of Israel, the king explained that he saw Jewish resettlement as a European problem, not an Arab one. Roosevelt promised to not take any action unless he conferred further with Abdul Aziz. A week later, President Roosevelt died. *

Abdul Aziz faced problems at home. Historically, the zealous fighters, the *Ikhwan,* whom the king had enlisted, renounced all signs of technological modernization and wealth because the items were considered anti-Islamic. They were pleased when the king threw out his phonograph set. Since the king's warrior force had expanded his rule, he rewarded them with land and published major works of their revered leader, Muhammed Al-Wahab. However, the *Ikhwan* turned on Aziz in 1929 when he made a business deal involving British tobacco, a taboo item. His new subjects helped him put down the rebellion. The conflict between the zealots and the royals continued through to the present day. *

Not long after we had signed our contracts, I was watching the early morning news and was stunned to learn there had been a bombing in eastern Saudi Arabia.

"Randy!" I yelled from the bottom of the steps in our living room. "Come down here!"

I heard his feet pound the hardwood floors above as he rolled out of bed. He tumbled quickly down the stairs, joined me in front of the TV and took a sip of coffee from my mug. Together we stared at the gray and grisly pictures of a bombed-out building. The reporter mentioned something about a U.S. military housing complex in Dharhan and "…a terrorist act believed to be the work of anti-American factions in Saudi Arabia." While the Saudi government insisted on controlling the investigation, the name of Osama Bin Laden surfaced as a potential

18

suspect. We were familiar with the name because of his alleged connections to previous bombings in Riyadh and Africa.

"Great," Randy sighed. "Now all of our friends are going to call and tell us what a terrible mistake we're making by going over there."

"Are we?" I asked.

Randy paused before responding. "Yeah, we're taking a risk. But with all the security around the royal family, we'll probably be safer there than here. Surely they'd look after us. Besides, buildings blow up here too."

"True, there's a lot of violence here, like the riots we worked through in Los Angeles," I said.

Suddenly the phone rang. Randy glanced at the clock and said, "Six a.m. I'll bet that's Mr. Al-Rasheed calling to see if we're going to chicken out. I'll get it."

He picked up the receiver. "Hello? Mr. Al-Rasheed? We thought that might be you."

I moved closer and tried to listen in.

"No, no, we were up," said Randy as I anxiously sipped my coffee. I could only hear Mr. Al-Rasheed's mumbled responses.

"Yes," continued Randy. "The Saudi consulate has been fine, and we have the plane tickets."

There was a moment of silence when I couldn't hear any garbled sound coming over the line. Finally the mumbling continued.

"Yes, we just heard about it on the news. Well, I'd be lying if I said we didn't have some concerns." Randy paused. "Well, you're probably right. Our own city streets are pretty violent."

'Oh, yes, I'd appreciate that. And thank the prince for apprising us. We'll talk again soon."

After Randy hung up, he explained that the prince had instructed Mr. Al-Rasheed to call and reassure us everything would be fine, and that we'd be perfectly safe in Saudi. The crime rate was much lower than the crime rate in America.

I was silent for a few moments as I pondered our predicament and reevaluated our decision.

"What do you think?" Randy asked finally.

"I'm not going to let a few angry people ruin a dream," I said with determination.

"The prince and princess have a great vision for their children. I'd like to be a part of it," he said.

"Then we'll go ahead with this?" I asked, searching his eyes for comfort.

He put his arms around me. "I think we can do some good there."

In Monterrey, we believed God in his providence was leading us. I agreed with Randy and felt my faith and confidence return. We decided that conflict would not dissuade us, but we also agreed to visit with Jack and Tyan when they returned to California for their summer vacations.

Later that spring Randy and I drove to the mountain community of Idyllwild to visit with Jack, Tyan and their daughter, Annina. I stood quietly on the redwood deck of their summer sanctuary admiring the tree-lined property and nearby meadow. A light vanilla fragrance from the tree trunks filled the air. Needles from the pine trees carpeted the forest floor. Translucent green leaves hanging from the limbs of white oaks created a canopy of shade over the yard and adjoining lane. Pale pink manzanita blossoms clung tenaciously to their burgundy and gray branches that twisted and turned as they stretched skyward. A bumble bee flew a lazy path to the indigo lupines that were wilting in the heat of the afternoon. Jack was barbecuing chicken and the pungent smell was tantalizing. Idyllwild was a special place for us because we had grown up there.

Jack said, "Life is very different in Saudi. You'll go through a lot of adjusting. After you've been there about six months, you'll realize you're not on vacation. That's when a lot of ex-pats go through some culture shock and depression."

"I can imagine," I said. "But the ho-hum of a nine-to-five job makes me restless."

"I understand."

Tyan joined us from the kitchen with a tray of lemonade. Annina followed close behind and climbed onto the bench. "At least Westerners live in compounds that separate you from the stress of the city. You can live a fairly normal life inside the walls. And you won't have to cover up either." Tyan handed Annina a glass of lemonade which she took gingerly.

Jack continued, "Dating is illegal, and the police make random road stops. Be sure you carry your papers with you at all times. If you get stopped, you'll have to prove you're legal residents and that you're married."

"You're kidding, right?" asked Randy.

"Oh, no," said Tyan. "We knew a devout couple from Lebanon that was stopped in Riyadh. They were hauled off to jail and questioned for hours because they didn't have their license with them. The husband was furious and said that had nothing to do with the heart of Islam and would never happen in Lebanon."

"So that's why Abdullah asked us to fax him a copy of our

marriage license?" asked Randy.

"Yup," said Jack as he tossed Randy a cold can of beer. "We had to do the same thing."

"Thanks," said Randy popping the lid open.

Tyan paused for a moment before saying, "You have a good contract don't you?"

"It looked reasonable," I said.

"And the prince's representative has been very good to us. In fact, I think he could become a good friend," said Randy.

"Well, the reason I ask is that Westerners don't always get paid for the work they do. I did a little tutoring for a young girl from a wealthy family and never got paid. They kept saying, 'next week.' I quit and said I would be back when they paid me. They never paid me so I never went back."

Jack added, "Well surely they can afford you. The rulers are billionaires now that they're selling so much oil. I read somewhere that Middle Eastern countries are virtually draining wealth from Western countries because we use so much of their oil. It's one of the biggest financial drains in history."

"I thought we learned to conserve oil back in the seventies," I said.

"We should have," said Tyan.

"We calculated our entire salary package," said Randy, "and figured that our package is the equivalent of seventy cents to them. I tip better than that!"

"Where did you find that information?" asked Jack.

"It was in a European financial paper. I keep up with all that stuff for our own portfolio."

"Are you still using your stock broker's license?" asked Tyan.

"Yeah, part-time. I work for a small company in San Gabriel."

Jack said, "Just be your self. The younger Saudis have traveled the world. They're very modern. Take a few side trips to nearby countries and think of the whole thing as a learning experience."

"Thanks for the suggestions," I said.

Tyan added, "And keep your blond hair covered. Stay with Randy or a large group of women and you'll be fine."

We visited a while longer and decided to get together the following summer to compare our experiences of teaching in foreign countries. As Randy and I drove off in our black Porsche, little Annina poked her head over the railing and ran down the steps waving good-bye. Jack scooped her up in his arms. We waved back and drove down the mountains toward home.

We continued our preparations over the summer. We got our visas through the Saudi embassy in Los Angeles. The dogs had all the necessary shots and paper work. We held a couple of gatherings in our home to say good bye to friends and family. At last we were packed and ready.

On a foggy morning in late August, I lingered on the second story balcony of our California home and looked around the verdant courtyard. The crimson brick walk lay silent, and the pink myrtles slept under the gray cover of dawn. Droopy white impatiens blossoms hung low and stretched their arms around huge tree trunks. Sleepy oaks lined the street, their laden boughs forming a shelter across the road. The slate green head of an occasional olive tree nodded undercover of the oak branches. Nature awaited the advent of day just as I awaited our journey overseas.

Randy lugged the suitcases out onto the walk while I grabbed the dogs by their leashes. They pranced down the walk toward the street. Randy slid open the van door and motioned for them to hop in. "Sometimes I think dogs have life all figured out. As long as they're with people who love them, they're content." He slammed the door shut and got behind the wheel. Before driving off down the street, we joined together in prayer.

"Dear Lord," I began, "please watch over our home in our absence and prepare a safe place for us in Saudi Arabia. Lead us in paths of righteousness for your name's sake."

"May your name be glorified, and let our journey be safe and successful," added Randy.

Unfortunately, the international terminal at the Los Angeles Airport was flooded with hundreds of travelers who waited impatiently in line as a handful of jaded ticket agents took their time checking bags and issuing boarding passes. We missed our flight to New York and took the next one, but making the connection to the international flight was stressful. The porter didn't think we'd make it but said a friend in baggage would help. He smiled when Randy offered them a huge tip.

We reached the check-in counter, and the attendant said that the plane was being held for a number of passengers. At last, Randy and I ran down the halls to the waiting 747. As I made my way down the aisle, I felt like we had already arrived in the Middle East. We walked through a sea of impenetrable black veils amid somber, bearded Arab faces. The sight of so many veiled women was unsettling. Even though Mr. Al-Rasheed had mentioned that the practice was meant to protect women, my research had revealed that women were frequently considered sexual predators. The covering was intended to conceal a woman's figure so she would no longer be viewed as provocative. *

Randy and I found our seats in front of a family and stored our carry-on baggage. As I sat down, I noticed the mother's coffee brown eyes peer between the narrow slit in her veil. I smiled, and after a brief instant, her eyes smiled back with a sparkle.

Randy sniffed the air. "What's that strange smell?"

"That's probably your dinner, dear," I whispered, patting him on the arm.

"Guess we won't be watching any good movies," Randy complained.

Trying to be positive I said, "Maybe we can relax and get some sleep."

"Well, I'm already beginning to regret this."

Because we had asked God for his guidance and had agreed on the venture, I met this complaint with icy silence. I had to admit, though, the trip had been stressful, and in the new environment, I suddenly felt quite alone. Perhaps my dreams had gotten the best of me. What were we doing taking this risk in the middle of our lives? Was God really leading us? I reminded myself that Randy and I had prayed, we were in agreement, and the door had opened. I also recalled something a retired friend had said. *My only regret is that I didn't take enough risks. I'll never know what I could have done.* Encouraged by her words, I looked around the cabin. I saw a few American businessmen. They sat quietly reading newspapers as if they were on a flight to just another American city, and I was reassured by their calm.

Movies were considered to be a venue of Western decadence laden with images. Since worshipping images was against Islam, I was surprised to see a large video screen. Following take-off though, I was more surprised when an Arab music video began playing. It featured a lead singer with a group of men sitting around a blazing desert fire singing and dancing. The men wore long white robes called *thobes* with red-and-white-checkered scarves called *ghutras*. The *ghutras* were held in place by a black band, an *igaal*. Before long, the singing and dancing became joyful and frenzied. They grabbed one another by the hands and circled the fire together. The Arab men had far more freedom to demonstrate physical closeness than Western men did.

After dinner the lights in the cabin were turned down. Our trip was uneventful until we were flying over the Arabian Peninsula some twelve hours later. Randy opened the window screen. I leaned over and looked toward the sea of caramel sand; the deep azure sky hung overhead.

"Guess we're not in the States anymore," he sighed, with an edge in his voice.

Confused by his change of attitude and lack of faith, I feared what he might say next and decided it was a good time to change into more conservative clothing. I grabbed my carry-on case and headed to the restroom. Inside, the floors were sopping wet since personal cleansing was done with a water hose rather than toilet paper. I was glad I had put my shoes back on and carried a packet of tissues with me. I changed into a long denim dress and returned to my seat.

On the approach to the airport, a desert wind suddenly slammed our plane toward the rippling waves of sand. Then, the wind slapped the plane down again. With clenched fists, I begged God to keep the plane in the air, and then looked at the family sitting behind me. Their faces were tense, but the eyes of the young mother whom I had noticed previously were empathic and kind. Though customs, religion and a black veil separated us, in that moment we looked into one another's eyes and understood each other. The pilot circled the airport again. The next approach to the airstrip was successful. When the tires hit the runway, a sigh of relief was heard throughout the cabin.

The international airport was named after one of the moderate and progressive kings, King Khalid. It was an impressive gateway to the desert kingdom. Luscious palms and ficus trees lined corridors and surrounded gurgling fountains like a desert oasis. Since Islam forbade portraiture as an art form, the geometric designs were intricate and striking. Crimson and navy mosaics with the eight-pointed Islamic star covered the tiled walls and floors. A domed ceiling with rows of tessellated triangles stretched overhead. Another dome was decorated with a spectacular blue and gold mosaic.

Hundreds of men from countries like Pakistan, India and the Philippines formed long lines at the customs gate. The men formed the bulk of the labor force in the kingdom and were looked down upon because of their low economic status. Waiting along the tiled walls were numerous Saudi men in their *thobes,* holding signs with the names of arriving guests. The noise and clamber of the hustle and bustle was draining after our long flight, and I longed for peace and quiet.

A tall gentleman in a crisp white *thobe* and *ghutra* approached us and politely introduced himself as Akbar Al-Jouri, an employee of Mr. Al-Rasheed. We were greatly relieved Abdullah had arranged for someone to assist us since we were both exhausted and overwhelmed. Mr. Al-Jouri was soft-spoken and had kind brown eyes, so we gave him our passports upon request and hoped he could shorten the customs process. Unfortunately, he learned that our luggage was in New York and wouldn't arrive for another week. We still needed to get the dogs, so he patiently escorted us toward baggage claim, where passengers from the East and the West gathered. Thin porters from developing countries were clad in drab green uniforms. They mingled amongst the passengers and searched incessantly for travelers needing assistance.

I sat on the rim of an empty luggage belt waiting anxiously for Aslan and Cheyenne to appear. A young woman draped in black sat down beside me and eagerly struck up a conversation.

"Why are you covered? It is hot outside and you are free," she said.

"I'm going to be working for a prince and princess and I don't want to offend them or cause any conflict."

"But you are free," she insisted.

I stared at her curiously because I had been instructed otherwise. Suddenly Randy called me to come and help him with the dogs.

"My husband needs me so I must help him," I said.

"Good luck to you in my country," she said.

I thanked her with admiration for her openness to speak with strangers.

Aslan and Cheyenne rode up the luggage belt looking frazzled in their crates. With their eyes still drooping from their sedating medication, they wagged their tails when they saw us. The porters backed away from the huge animals until my husband pulled out some *riyals,* or Saudi currency. The *riyals* must have been worth a lot for suddenly a dozen porters surrounded Randy. He pointed arbitrarily to two men who then lifted the dog crates onto carts. Though I'd heard outlandish stories about Saudi's customs procedures, we quietly followed Mr. Al-Jouri through simple and routine inspections.

When we approached the exit, someone called us by name. "Mr. and Mrs. Decker! Welcome to Saudi Arabia!"

Randy and I glanced at one another and then at an older American couple donning cherubic smiles. "Do we know you?" asked Randy.

The tall gray-haired gentleman said, "I'm George Phelps, and this is my wife, Lydia. We wanted to meet you on your first overseas assignment. We teach at a palace school like yours, but we have your students' cousins."

I extended my hand toward the charming woman and said, "It's wonderful to meet you. I had no idea there were two schools for royal students."

Lydia said, "There are several more, actually. Americans stick together overseas. Our villa is just around the corner from yours, so we'll be neighbors. And don't worry about the dogs. Akbar will bring them. He's become a dear friend of ours, and we can assure you of his dependability."

Mr. Al-Jouri nodded toward Randy. "Sir, I bring your things. Go with Mr. Phelps."

I marveled at the times that we had put our lives into the hands of strangers lately, but something about this couple's demeanor was trustworthy, and I thanked God for the warm welcome and assistance in a strange land.

George grabbed our carry-on bags and said, "Akbar's from India and supports his aging parents back home. He went to college but can't get a job in India. He's happy to be a driver."

George led us to the parking lot, saying he could probably answer some of our questions. Randy admitted that he'd had concerns about money since we had fronted a lot to get there. George had too and offered to show Randy how to submit receipts for reimbursement. George pulled slowly out of the airport onto a modern highway. Since the sun had set while we were inside, we could see little beyond the lights.

Randy asked, "Tell me, George, we like Mr. Al-Rasheed, but what's he really like?"

"He's great. Being positive about the host culture helps new arrivals adjust, especially since Saudi Arabia is so different from other countries. We were here last year and think you'll love this job."

"Then I can sleep tonight," sighed Randy.

Lydia laughed and told him to expect a bout with jet lag. Apparently, the best way to handle it was to get up and go about our business. Before we knew, it would be over.

Within half an hour we turned onto a dirt road that led to an isolated walled community referred to as a compound. When we parked beside the security office, a security guard appeared with a flashlight and a long stick with a mirror attached at the end. He circled our vehicle and checked under the hood. At last the security guard motioned for us to proceed, and the large wrought iron gate rolled back.

As we entered the enormous residential community, Randy let out a slow whistle. "Geez, is this Saudi Arabia or Palm Springs?" The grounds were meticulously landscaped. Lighted palm trees lined the entryway, and neatly mowed lawns surrounded Mediterranean styled homes. White vincas and yellow marigolds trimmed green lawns and burst over the edges of large clay pots and planters. Red bougainvilleas crawled up carports, porches and arbors. Leafy ferns and philodendron dangled from hanging planters on peaceful front porches. A large tiled fountain with soft lighting sat on a mound of green grass where the road diverged into separate housing tracts. A small business center had a grocery store, hair salon, cleaners and restaurant. The restaurant overlooked a spectacular pool with several large fountains. A huge deck with several striped cabanas and matching lounge chairs surrounded the pool. George drove by a tennis court where several couples were playing under bright lights. He pointed to a gym with a spa, bowling alley and private theater.

When we parked in front of our villa, I got out and studied the two-story, stucco building with rock gardens and towering palm trees. Apart from a dry, warm, desert breeze that rustled through the palm fronds above, everything was enveloped by peaceful quiet. I felt the tension of the trip and my worries ease out of my body.

Thank you, Lord, I prayed silently, *for such a beautiful home away from home.*

Randy and Akbar gently lowered the dog crates from the back of the truck and opened them. Since the pavement was still holding the heat of a desert day, they could hardly set their paws on it. They scuttled quickly to the nearest tuft of grass. They followed us as we went up the walk and entered the villa. George and Lydia led us on a quick tour, pointing to the modern features and amenities throughout. Our new home was decorated with traditional Western furnishings, and the kitchen had all the necessary modern conveniences and appliances including a washer, dryer and dishwasher.

"Unfortunately, modernization has upset the clerics and caused tension for the royals, but we'll have plenty of time to explain that," said George. "Tomorrow we'd like to take you downtown for your first exposure to the country."

Lydia added, "And you'll need an *abaya* right away, Kristin."

We agreed, so George offered to pick us up in the morning. He also wanted us to meet an American teaching couple, Mike and Jan Barker, whom he had hired to teach at his school. They had lived in a number of foreign countries. Lydia thought that the six of us could support one another through the adjustment period and have some fun exploring new places and restaurants at the same time.

After we said good night, Randy and I sauntered upstairs to the huge master bedroom with the dogs following close behind. They jumped onto the king-sized bed as we walked out onto a small balcony.

Randy gazed at the sparkling expanse of stars overhead. The palms swayed gently with the desert breezes. Together, we marveled at the beauty of God's creation.

"I've always wanted to see the stars from the desert like Abraham, Isaac and Jacob did . . . and Ishmael," said Randy.

"Yes, Ishmael, the son of Abraham and Sara's maid, Hagar," I said, recalling how Sara had sent Hagar from their camps. Hagar had boasted about having a son while Sara remained barren. Upon her expulsion,

Hagar cried out to God. He heard her lonely prayer in the desert, provided water for her and promised her descendants as numerous as a nation. Indeed, a memorial commemorating God's provision to Hagar had been erected in the holy city of Mecca.

"I believe Arabs are the people of the promise to Hagar," said Randy.

"I do too. Christians study the Hebrew culture because of our heritage in the Old Testament and the prophecies about Messiah. But in some way, God has his stamp upon these people too. We need to learn more about them."

Randy put his arms around me. "I also think we can make a nice home here. I heard everything I needed to hear from George. I'm glad to know he likes Abdullah so much."

"Me too, and Akbar seems like a great person. Guess we'll be busy tomorrow, so let's get some rest," I suggested.

Back inside, we shoved the dogs to the foot of the bed and dropped into it completely exhausted. I was at peace knowing that God had not only provided an exciting adventure that was a dream of a lifetime, he had providentially guided us to a safe place where we could flourish. He had already provided us with friends and mentors who would help us learn about an entirely different way of life. I felt full of divine purpose and direction, realizing Randy and I could make a worthy contribution in a tenuous and transitioning part of the world.

3.

WOMEN IN BLACK

AN UNFAMILIAR WAIL woke me at dawn on our first morning in Saudi Arabia. The male voice of the *muezzin,* or crier, boomed over the loud speaker of a nearby mosque for the first prayer of the day. The *muezzin* called believers to kneel, face Mecca, and recite a *salut,* or prayer, five times a day. Randy and I had to be up early anyway, so we dragged ourselves downstairs.

Usually I would spend time reading my Bible and praying. Since we weren't allowed to bring our own Bibles, I prayed and meditated on passages from Psalm Twenty-three that I had memorized. Knowing God was my shepherd and would lead me along green pastures and quiet streams was comforting as I prepared to face a different way of life. I could imagine him walking beside me.

Over our morning cup of coffee, I wondered aloud what it would be like to live by a moral code that enforced strict obedience and gender segregation. We'd be traveling into the center of Riyadh, so I was about to witness the effects firsthand. Hopefully, it wouldn't mar my own self-perception or dampen my enthusiasm about making a positive contribution.

When George and Lydia arrived, Lydia handed me an a*baya* and scarf and helped me adjust them about my neck. Reluctantly, I tucked wisps of blonde hair under the heavy scarf and frowned at my strange profile in the mirror. Fortunately, I didn't have to cover my face.

When I tried walking, I tripped over the hem. "Does it have to be black?" I asked, lifting the hem up slightly and hoping I'd find something more flattering than the drab black robe.

"In Saudi it does. It's the most fundamental Islamic state," she said. "At least you don't have to wear it in your home or around the compound."

I nodded in agreement, grabbed my purse and followed her to the car. Outside, George introduced Jan and Mike Barker. They were world travelers who had taught in South America, Africa and Europe. In Saudi, they would be teaching the cousins of our students along with George and Lydia. Since they had recently arrived, Jan also needed to shop for an *abaya*. She was a tall, intelligent blonde who bemoaned the idea of covering with the black veil and *abaya*.

When we left the compound and turned onto a narrow dirt road, I was surprised to see how bleak and barren the surrounding desert was. Natural vegetation was sparse. Huge mounds of sand, rock and rubble left from the construction of our compound dotted the landscape.

Shortly we passed *Imam University,* a large campus for young men training to be religious leaders. Male students in white *thobes* and prayer caps walked soberly to and from class. Across the street was an obstacle course with military style training equipment. It seemed out of place in the religious setting, so Lydia explained that the first King's warriors were religious zealots known as the *Ikhwan*. Though King Abdul Aziz kept their identity a secret to the outside world, their brutal war tactics were well known inside the kingdom. They followed the radical teachings of Al-Wahab and reconciled religion with the use of violence by thinking that the ends justified the means. The *Ikhwan* warriors provoked great fear among many neighboring tribes and caused an immediate conversion to the Wahabbi form of Islam. When the warriors turned on Abdul Aziz, he squashed their rebellion without mercy, but their ideal picture of what Islam should become remained among the people. *

George also warned us to be careful when driving by the university because he knew compound residents who had been harassed and forced off the road by zealous students. This confused me as well because I considered Islam to be a religion of peace. In fact, the name Islam meant peace or submission. However, the place of peace, or *Dar-es-Salam*, was reserved only for those of the Muslim faith. Nonbelievers were said to exist in a state of conflict called *Dar Al-Harb*. The two abodes were thought to be in a constant strife with one another until *Dar es-Salam* consumed *Dar Al-Harb*. *

Most modern Muslims considered thoughtful persuasion an effective conduit from *Dar Al-Harb* to *Dar es-Salam,* but a radical group of believers had arisen in Egypt during the 1980s. The followers of Abd Al-Salam Faraj preached a sixth and often forgotten pillar of Islam, *Jihad.* This pillar justified violence and deceit as acceptable means to defend and advance Islam. Under the leadership of Faraj, the group had been responsible for the assassination of the Egyptian leader, Anwar Sadat. Faraj was tried and executed for his crime. * Upon learning of this radical interpretation of *Jihad*, Randy and I decided we'd feel safer taking an alternate route for our travels into the city.

Our compound was on the perimeters of the city, but we soon reached a paved highway. Huge homes in earthen colors with high concrete walls were under construction everywhere. Some homes were landscaped with aqua blue palms and rosy bougainvilleas that spread their branches and blossoms over the fortress like walls. Driveway entrances were framed with intricate bronze and black gates that allowed us to catch a glimpse of curved driveways lined with palms. Camel and goat hair tents the color of Turkish coffee were set up among the new building sites where realtors could conduct their business. Since the land belonged to the royal family, only princes could execute real estate deals. Mosques, with their oval domes and towering minarets, were also being built close to the new housing tracts.

Workers from developing countries scurried about the one and two acre sites. Since Saudi Arabia had distinctly defined social classes, the workers were considered the bottom of the social rung and were looked down upon by the elite wealthy class and burgeoning middle class.

Before we reached the city center, we stopped at a popular outdoor shopping center, or s*ouk*. One storefront after another lined the hot cement walkways like an open-air mall. We strode along a maze of sidewalks passing fine fabric stores, brass shops, china shops, carpet and houseware stores and shoe stores. An occasional stench of sewer wafted through the warm dry air making us cover our mouths and cough. Soon, the temperature would reach 120 degrees.

"How can these people work in the heat?" I asked.

"It's pretty controversial. When the temperatures rises over 120, outdoor labor is supposed to stop," Lydia said.

"What we've learned," added George, "is that the temperature never officially rises above 120."

"What do you mean?" I asked.

"What we mean is that if you want to know the real temperature in Riyadh, don't check with Saudi officials. Read the temperatures that are sighted on bank displays from other countries, like the Saudi English bank."

"So if it reaches 140, these people are still working construction?" asked Randy.

"That's right," said George.

I could hardly believe that workers were treated with such disdain and wondered why unions hadn't helped the laborers.

We found a cluster of *abaya* shops and entered one. Inside were endless racks and stacks of black robes and scarves. As Lydia and I rummaged through them, Jan stared at the piles and looked defeated. She hated wasting money on an *abaya*. Though I understood her sentiments, I thought I'd cope more effectively if I wore a nice one. I searched for silk covers among the racks of polyester, but silk abayas cost nearly a hundred dollars. Lydia thought I could probably find a polyester *abaya* embroidered with attractive gold thread for around thirty dollars.

Jan shook her head in despair. "I just want the cheapest one I can find."

"Try thinking of them as choir robes or a judge's robe," Lydia said winking at me.

"Mike and I have lived all over the world, but this is the most challenging time I've had adjusting to a foreign culture," said Jan.

Lydia gave Jan an empathic smile and explained that the wearing and shedding of the *abaya* was a challenge for Western women. In public, we were expected to cover fully or encounter lascivious looks, and sometimes acts, from men who probably considered us prostitutes.

We wandered through more shops discussing the advantages of each kind of *abaya*. Some snapped, some zipped and some tied in a knot at the neck. Though many were simple and plain, nearly all of them had matching scarves that were trimmed with beautiful embroidery and shiny beads. Occasionally we'd find a scarf with dangling gold beads or coins giving it a mystical flair.

Neither Jan nor I found an *abaya* that we could tolerate, so George drove toward a shopping center downtown. He explained that some twenty-five years before, most of the roads were dirt and that huge packs of wild dogs often roamed them. Randy and I marveled at the quick-paced development that had created the modern scene unfolding before us. We passed office supply stores, bookstores, banks, hotels and several art and craft stores. A carpet store displayed gorgeous rugs from Asia and Persia in the windows.

George pointed out fine restaurants with fare from countries like China, Thailand, Japan and Lebanon as well as fast food restaurants like Kentucky Fried Chicken and McDonald's. As long as Western companies abode by *Sharia* law, the religious law of Wahabbi Islam, and provided a separate entrance for women and children, the companies were allowed to do business in the country. The women's side had a separate counter for ordering and individual booths that were surrounded with high walls and curtains. Inside the private booths, families could eat together and the women could take off their veils. Shortly, we drove by an Italian coffee shop where a few Arab men were sitting around an outdoor patio. They were sipping coffee and casually reading the morning paper. In the window, a sign in Arabic and English read, *No Ladies Allowed.*

A multi-story mall with dark tinted windows stretched the length of a block. We parked and entered the upscale shopping center. Air conditioning blasted throughout the corridors and plazas. Palm and ficus trees surrounded colorful tiled fountains that flowed peacefully. Polished marble floors were inlaid with intricate geometric patterns. The atmosphere in the mall was so refreshing that I felt like I was wandering in a desert oasis.

We wandered into an *abaya* shop where I found an attractive silk cover and scarf. The silk had an aura of elegance in the way it gracefully fell from my shoulders and draped around my sandals. Embroidered black roses trimmed with shiny black beads decorated the shoulders and back. Matching roses bordered the edges of the sheer scarf. The beauty and sheen of the soft, flowing silk helped me retain some dignity. To save money, Jan bought a plain one.

Jan and I were eager to explore our new surroundings before jet lag overwhelmed us. We strolled down the long corridors discovering fabric shops, antique stores, shoe stores, cosmetic stores, perfumeries, incense shops, pharmacies and boutiques. A small food court with fast food chains was located on an upper level.

As noon approached, more and more Arab families filled the mall. Women were either with a male family member or a large group of women. Some Arab women covered their faces with a veil, but others peered out from behind a narrow slit around their eyes. Apart from high heels, painted toes, gold bangles and embroidery, not a single feminine feature was visible.

Glancing around Lydia commented, "The *Qur'an* teaches that women only need to dress modestly and cover their bosom, but Saudis seem to be influenced by tradition as well. Saudi women are covered from head to toe in black only, like the *Bedouin* women who used to roam the deserts in the past. It's considered as protection for women."

"Protection from what?" Jan challenged.

"There's a lot of talk about men having special needs," Lydia said. "I know an American woman who was shopping for groceries and hadn't bothered to cover her hair. Suddenly, a Saudi exposed himself to her. Then he taunted her, saying there wasn't a thing she could do about it since she hadn't covered her hair. If she called the authorities, he'd claim that she'd provoked him. The woman was disgusted of course. I don't think she ever shopped there again."

I shared an incident that my sister-in-law, Tyan, had related when we last visited in California. She and my brother taught in Riyadh during the Gulf War of 1991. Since Tyan was six months pregnant, they stopped at the Kuwaiti *Souk* after work to buy a crib. Tyan didn't bother to cover her blond hair and entered a furniture store while my brother waited in the car. Once inside, she asked a Pakistani clerk if the store carried cribs. He directed her to the second story where she could clearly see additional furniture. When she reached the top of the stairs though, she didn't see any cribs. He motioned for her to follow him further, which she did. As she peered around a corner, she saw a mattress laying flat on the floor. When he tried to throw her onto it, she screamed and pushed him to the ground. He was stunned by her refusal and strength. She turned and fled downstairs toward the manager, yelled at him and explained what had happened. In order to prevent a scene and a nasty encounter with the religious police, the manager apologized and escorted her out of the store. If the police had been involved, she'd have been blamed for the incident. She warned me to never go anywhere alone.

"Has anyone thought men might be able to practice self-control?" asked Jan rather sarcastically.

Randy added, "I'm offended by the idea that men can't control themselves."

George added, "But notice the Saudi men are dressed as conservatively as the women in long white *thobes* and those checkered head scarves."

Two bearded Arabs strolled by hand in hand. "Are those two men?" I began.

"No, it means they're very good friends," said George. "People outside of the States are more comfortable with physical closeness."

"So, that's why we had to cover up?" quipped Jan.

"I meant among the members of the same sex," explained George apologetically.

I admired Jan's witty spirit and looked forward to getting to know her better.

Lydia wanted to show Jan and me the jewelry stores since they were unlike anything in America. Lydia assured me that a group of women whose husbands were nearby would be safe. Our husbands wanted to browse in an electronics store, so together we women drifted from store to store entranced by the dazzling window displays of shimmering twenty-two karat gold and brilliant white diamonds. The diamond sets often ran into the hundreds of thousands of dollars, some into the millions of dollars. The high-end items were a result of the long established gold and diamond trade with African nations and revealed the immense wealth consumers in the oil-producing nation had accrued.

Lydia led us into a gold store and pointed out dozens of rows stacked with some fifty gold bracelets each. The angular cuts in the gold cast shimmering reflections of light. In the next cabinet, an enchanting diamond and sapphire bracelet caught my eye. It was about four thousand dollars and I let myself admire it longingly, thinking it would be a good way to reward myself for having to cover and sacrifice my personal freedoms. Perhaps I could buy it when we left Saudi, or on second thought, were jewels and wealth a means men used to seduce women into silent subservience and second-class status?

While we were window-shopping, the stores closed for *zuhr,* the noon prayer. The chanting voice of the *muezzin* once again vibrated through the loudspeakers. Shop doors slammed shut. Slat board shutters rolled down over many store windows; iron gates were pulled across the remaining stores. Business ground to a halt. While most men headed to the nearby mosque, some sat on a bench smoking or stared into a store window. Many veiled women meandered about the mall.

Lydia explained that women were encouraged to pray in the privacy of their own homes and that daily prayer was only one of the Five Pillars of Islam. Four additional practices were required of Muslims; the giving of alms, or *zakat;* recitation of the *Shahada* confession, '*There is no god but God and Mohammed is his prophet;*' fasting, or *saum,* during Ramadan; and a pilgrimage, or *Hajj,* to Mecca at least once during a lifetime. *

Within minutes, a police patrol approached our area. The stern religious policeman, or *mutawwa,* held a camel prod tightly in his hand and was wearing a long, sweeping, brown robe and had a gray beard. The *mutawwain* were responsible to the clerics as well as the powerful Prince of Riyadh, Salman. They were also known as, 'The Committee for the Suppression of Vice and Propagation of Virtue.' * A somber civil policeman who accompanied the *mutawwa* slung a heavy machine gun over his shoulder. Side by side, the two men marched down the center of the mall scouring the premises for offenders who were neither attending prayer nor covering their hair.

Terrified by their ominous appearance, I turned quickly away and stared into a store window. I pulled my silk scarf tighter around my hair and longed to crawl into a hole and hide as the policemen passed directly behind me shouting. Soon the men had gone on to the next section.

Our three husbands rushed toward us. "Did you see them?" Randy asked me.

"Briefly," I said, relieved that he was by my side. He pointed down the long corridor.

"Cover!" yelled the *mutawwa* at one Filipina woman and then another. The women lifted their scarves in obedience and covered their long, dark tresses.

"Cover!" came the vociferous order again as the *mutawwa* pointed at each woman.

"Unlike the Apostle Paul of the New Testament who taught that hair is a woman's covering, the clerics think hair is erotic," explained George.

Lydia added, "During the Gulf War, the *mutawwain* were enraged when they saw our military women uncovered in public and walking alongside of male soldiers. The clerics considered them a corrupting influence on Islamic women."

George continued, "There were rumors that a fatality occurred after some kind of confrontation between an unveiled female soldier and a *mutawwa*. When she didn't cover, the *mutawwa* charged her. I guess she thought he was a terrorist and fired on him. Stories like that spread like wildfire among Western compounds but never get into the local news."

He reminded us of a famous incident that did make international headlines. Forty-seven Saudi women dismissed their chauffeurs and drove a convoy of cars through downtown Riyadh. Even though there was no law at the time against women driving, the women were arrested and accused of renouncing Islam, an offense punishable by death. The women, many of them academics at King Saud University, were banned from working and stripped of their passports. Some even received death threats. *

The driving incident prompted Sheik Bin Baz, the highest-ranking religious figure in Saudi, to issue a *fatwa* and declare it was illegal for women to drive. Many Westerners believed that the crackdown on Arab women was a political ploy on the part of the royal family to distract the fundamental clerics and critics from obsessing over half a million U.S. troops arriving on sacred Saudi soil.

George further explained that the royal family walks a fine line. King Faisal courageously introduced a number of financial and social reforms to the Kingdom. Encouraged by the late President John F. Kennedy in 1962, Faisal abolished slavery. Faisal next convinced the conservative clerics that television could be used for the expansion of Islam, and he opened the first television station in Riyadh. Protests that turned violent erupted at the opening of the station. An ultra-conservative prince, Prince Khalid ibn Musa'id, led the riot. A

36

policeman shot the leader during the demonstration. * The family of the young Musa'id never forgot nor forgave the incident.

Like King Faisal, the next king, Khalid bin Abdul Aziz, implemented social and political reforms, but he died of a heart attack in 1982. The fourth son of Abdul Aziz to ascend the throne was Crown Prince Fahad, son of Hassa bint Sudeiri. Fahad had served as Minister of Education and had been involved with governing for many years. He was a moderate familiar with two colliding worlds, the West and the Middle East. While he referred to himself as the Custodian of the Two Most Holy Mosques of Mecca and Medina, he also had a reputation of being wild and decadent from his days spent in the West. The first Gulf War erupted while Fahad was king. Though King Fahad and Crown Prince Abdullah agreed to allow U.S. troops to arrive on Saudi soil and protect the kingdom from a possible invasion, rumors circulated that indicated King Fahad and Crown Prince Abdullah, a more conservative Islamist, had heated, and sometimes violent clashes. *

The royal family has wanted to move the country forward cautiously, but has also had to put down open rebellion several times within the country, including one rebellion at the mosque in Mecca. King Faisal used force to protect the innocent pilgrims at the mosque and capture the violent zealots. The royals consult with the clerics when such events transpire, in order to obtain legitimacy for their actions. They also give the religious police a long leash, but many clerics think its a compromise and continue to criticize the royals. The princes battle constant rumors of debauchery, decadence, prostitution and drug use as their affluence increases, and they encounter modernization and Western civilization.

Once the *mutawwa* left, everyone returned calmly to his or her business, and the foreign women uncovered their heads. After prayer, the stores reopened. We entered an electronics store and Randy asked a clerk to hear a stereo system. The clerk explained that he must go next door and find a disc for demonstration. He used to have one, but the *mutawwa* came in one day, said his music was too loud and took his discs.

"Well, did he pay for them?" Randy asked.

The clerk cracked a smile and shook his head no.

While waiting for the clerk to return, I surveyed the packaged CDs. I noticed heavy black marks drawn all over the covers. When I looked more closely, I realized that the marks were drawn between men and women, and that the bare skin of women was blackened out. I picked up the CD for the musical score of *Immortal Beloved,* and saw that the arms, neck and cleavage of the lovely actress had been completely blackened over. I was dismayed that such beauty had been dismissed, distorted and despised.

Lydia told us that all Western materials, including newspapers, magazines, CDs and so forth, were censored by the clerics before being distributed to the Saudi public. Workers took black markers and crossed out anything considered objectionable, including ads for alcoholic beverages and cigarettes. Sometimes it took days for a newspaper or magazine to hit the stands. The news was rarely delivered on time.

Randy finally bought a player and we walked back into the mall. I started to enter a donut shop but saw a sign in bold red letters reading, *No Ladies Allowed.* I thought about sending Randy inside to buy a donut for me, but since I had witnessed the extent of gender segregation for myself, I decided the store didn't deserve my business at that time or any time in the future.

Shortly, we entered a stationery shop that displayed a huge assortment of post cards. Amidst photos of magnificent Moorish structures, palms, mosques, camels, and valiant men riding horses over the crests of sand dunes, I found a post card with a beautiful *Bedouin* woman draped in black and gold. Her brown eyes peered out from behind a gold-beaded cap that held her veil in place. Her eyes were friendly and yet as mysterious as the deep, dark midnight sky and caused me to wonder what it was like to be a woman of Arabia. What happiness did she find, and what sorrows or secrets cast their long shadows across her life? How did she cope with restrictions that isolated her from others and kept her from becoming all that she could be?

Suddenly, I discovered that I feared looking into her eyes. A terrifying reflection of my distant self emerged and replaced her image. I quickly repressed visions of anger, hatred and violence and forced myself to close my eyes and turn away. Believing that I'd had enough exposure to a lifestyle that destroyed the dignity of women, I suggested that we return to the comfort of our modern compound. Besides, jet lag was beginning to take its toll and I wanted to nap for the rest of the afternoon.

At home, the dogs greeted us enthusiastically. Randy plopped down on the sofa and flipped on the satellite television. I hung the *abaya* carelessly on a coat rack and walked upstairs. The dogs followed me and jumped onto the bed as I lay down. I tried to fall asleep, but the image of the *Bedouin* woman kept drifting across my mind causing me to struggle with buried and painful feelings of emotional imprisonment. Why had the picture triggered such unsettled feelings and images? Frightened, I pushed them out of my mind again and meditated on my worth as a redeemed child of God through faith. Grateful that I didn't have to comply with a rigid list of rules or struggle to gain his favor, I asked God to grant me his peace. The vivid green pastures and quiet streams I'd meditated upon from Psalm Twenty-three in my morning devotions drifted through my consciousness. I imagined the Lord walking calmly beside me as my shepherd. I knew I'd have to create my own internal place of safety where I could experience the Lord's peace and restoration. I snuggled up to my dogs, put my arm around Cheyenne and my toes against Aslan's soft back. I could hear Randy laughing downstairs. His voice comforted me, and at last sleep overcame me.

4.

POLITICS IN PARADISE

OVER THE COURSE of the next week, Randy and I struggled with jet lag and settled into our new home. I couldn't wait to tour the school and was excited when George made the arrangements for our first visit. The school was in the middle of the palace district where numerous walled palaces lined dusty paved roads. They were like fortresses emanating wealth and dignity as well as an apparent need for security and privacy. While luscious palms, acacias and eucalyptus trees gracefully draped their branches over the tops of the walls, security cameras were posted at intervals among them. Beside each gated entrance was a small room where guards waited all day. I wondered why there was so much security.

George explained that the royals remembered the fate of the Shah of Iran because they had plenty of enemies in their own country. One of their most caustic critics arose following the 1990 Iraqi invasion of Kuwait. A Saudi warrior from the Afghanistan war, Osama Bin Laden, had fought off invading infidels from Russia. When American troops landed on sacred Islamic soil to fight Saddam Hussein, Bin Laden offered to have his warriors fight. King Fahad refused the offer, and Bin Laden blatantly criticized the king. He became such an outspoken critic and menace, that in 1995 the Saudi government kicked Bin Laden out of the country. * He fled to the Sudan before returning to Afghanistan, though it was rumored that conservative members of the family secretly supported Bin Laden.

The patriarch of the Bin Laden family, Mohamed, accrued unbelievable wealth from the construction business he built during the 1960s and 1970s. He frequently worked for the royals and renovated the holy site of Mecca. Because of this great wealth, it was believed that Osama financed a number of terrorist attacks, including the recent attack on the Khobar military barracks in the eastern province of

40

Dhahran we had heard about on the news. *

I asked George, "Why does Bin Laden think we're infidels?"

"Our worldviews are entirely different. I don't think they understand us any more than we understand them."

"But don't you think we're all the same inside?" I asked.

"Well sure, but we haven't had the same education or been taught to look at things in the same way. The reasoning process is different."

George reminded us that the majority of Islamic scholars had not engaged in debates rooted in Greek or Roman philosophy, as had European and American philosophers and theologians. Muslim scholars had their own wealth and history of thought and debate. Islamic scholars established a worldview based on the revelation written in the *Qur'an,* the *Hadith,* a collection of anecdotal sayings about the life of the prophet Mohammed, and the varying schools of Islamic law. *Sharia* law, or the ideal religious law, provided guidelines for moral living for all of humanity and pervaded daily life of all faithful Muslims. Because there was no concept of original sin and humans were considered innocent, correct behavior was emphasized over correct belief. The Five Pillars of Islam comprised the core of Islamic behavior. Failure to act in accordance with these pillars of faith could cause great personal and familial shame.

Though the period of time preceding Mohammed the prophet had some exposure to both Christian and Judaic thought, the strains of Christianity that filtered into the desert were aberrant. Isolated in the Arabian deserts for centuries, Islam developed more austerely than in other countries. A well-known teacher of the seventeenth century, Mohammed Al-Wahab, studied a tenth century teacher named Al-Hanbal who considered reasoning to be evil. As a result, his followers adhered strictly to the literal interpretation of the *Qur'an.* They considered asceticism a sign of utmost holiness and forbade singing, dancing, music and congregating of the sexes. They also taught that modern innovations like the telephone and phonograph, great wealth and the mystical sect of Islam, *Sufism,* were signs of corruption. Wahabbi Islam retained a place for absolutes, but it also held tightly onto legalism with its rigid interpretation of the world and one's role in it. Following the Hanbalites, the Wahabbis emphasized rote memorization of the *Qur'an* in their public schools and spread the schools beyond the borders of Saudi into neighboring countries like Afghanistan.

Abdul Aziz was fond of explaining the Wahabbi preoccupation with technology by using the sword as an analogy. * The sword itself was neutral in value. It could be used for either good or bad. Its worth

41

was determined by the way it was used. In Northern Africa, St. Augustine of Hippo, fourth century church father and scholar, made the same point using money rather than the sword. Neutral in their essence, it was the use of the items that determined the worth. It also revealed the heart of the one who used them.

George explained, "People often reason differently in this part of the world. I think the absence of critical thinking in Saudi school curriculums produces citizens who can't usually distinguish fact from fantasy. With the emphasis on rote learning from the *Qur'an,* there is little room for the study of the languages, literature or science. Some of the royals have worked hard to change that too."

"What do they think about Greek philosophers like Aristotle or Plato, or science for that matter?"

George said, "Some *imams* are completely against teaching science altogether, and it wasn't long ago when the leading *imam* announced the world was flat. Some even questioned our landing on the moon as a Hollywood stunt."

Randy said, "I guess they had to retract that when Saudi sent up its own astronaut." *

"You bet," said George. "But those two statements show how wide the spectrum of thought can be. Even the princess told us not to spend more than two weeks studying Ancient Greece. You'll also encounter a more fatalistic world-view, so you'll hear people saying, '*Ensh'Allah,*' meaning, *As God wills.* People see time as rushing toward them, a phenomenon over which they have no control or input. In fact, it's against Islam to predict the future."

In addition, George suggested that fundamentalists considered us infidels because they had been primarily exposed to the visible train of Western thought, the rationalistic and the humanistic perspectives. Similar to the Russians who were fought in Afghanistan, Westerners were perceived as godless, selfish and vain imperialists. George had also read a news article about one of the convicted bombers of the World Trade Center in 1993. Mahmud Abouhalima admitted that he was sick of the secularism in the West because it kept people from understanding religion. *

"As a whole, we do have a level of spiritual illiteracy today," said Randy.

"After studying theology I've come to the same conclusion," I said.

But the modern Western worldview was not easily understood by casual observance. It had a long and complex history, but I reflected upon a brief outline to aid my own understanding. From the first century, the Roman Catholic churches preserved learning in the monasteries. Scribes and monks like Tertullian and Augustine were the educated elite and kept the lamp of learning alive by copying sacred manuscripts as well as various Latin and Greek classics. Truth was rooted in revelation, according to the Old and New Testaments. Slowly, the word of the church began to take pre-eminence over the scriptures, and that set the stage for the next theological development.

In the thirteenth century, the great Catholic theologian, Thomas Aquinas, taught that though the will of humankind was fallen and sinful, mankind's ability to reason clearly was still in tact. * He adapted the deterministic teachings of Aristotle to the Christian faith with the assumption that uncorrupted reason could lead individuals to truth and to a clear definition of reality. While Aquinas believed ultimate truth lay with God, other thinkers and scholars began to leave the fold of faith and grace to find reasonable and meaningful explanations of life.*

The dialogue of philosophers extended through the centuries to modern times with each thinker adding his own perspectives and modifications. Religious perspectives typically took the forms of either deism, which taught that God created the world and left it to operate without Him, or pantheism, which purported that God was in and throughout nature but unknowable personally. Grace, faith and spirituality played a declining role in the explanations of the universe, God, humankind in the universe and their relations with everything else.

During the Renaissance and the Enlightenment, the classical Greek philosophers were studied widely. The exaltation of man's reasoning came to fruition. What was true and what wasn't true became a point of contentious argument. Eventually, philosophers decided that people created their own truths at the expense of absolute and revealed truths. The long-term result was that rationalistic and humanistic philosophy impacted the modern world with a point of view that permeated Western culture, including its educational institutions, politics and the arts.

According to Plato, the teacher of Aristotle, the absence of absolutes or universals that result from a strictly rational world left no room for meaning, value or spirituality. It also left many modern individuals despairing their own existence and looking for something, someone or some great experience to give life meaning and validate his or her existence. In an attempt to assuage the sorrow of despair, not every choice made was a healthy and productive one. Many times, choices were destructive. Perhaps choices of desperation that individuals made presented the rest of the world with an eclipsed and altered view of the Western conscience.

While Islamic scholars rejected humanism, so did an entire segment of Western society. The pervading Western worldview didn't represent all people of the West. While many a Western thinker believed reconciliation of faith and reason to be impossible as well as intellectual suicide, other scholars challenged this position. Interestingly enough, the Reformation was occurring in Northern Europe at about the same time the Renaissance was occurring in Italy. * Reformation scholars like Luther and Calvin reintegrated faith and reason and rejected humanism as contrary to scriptures. They believed a world without faith in Christ to be a world of futility and despair. They changed the equation of medieval scholars by saying that once faith occurred, reason would then make sense of the world and all its elements.

I said, "I value critical thinking, but it doesn't override my faith. We can use our minds to understand and explain the world around us."

George said, "Yes, just put the horse *before* the cart, and a whole new world opens. For Westerners, it comes down to where you think knowledge and truth come from, reason or revelation. In other words, does it come from man or God?"

"So, much of the West looks to science, reason and human experience as a source of knowledge, but the Middle East looks to revelation and God."

"I think so," said George. "And each side feels threatened by the other. I wish we wouldn't take disagreement over the different positions as a personal insult or criticism."

"I hope we can create respect in our private schools. Maybe that'll help diplomacy in the future," I said.

Randy asked, "But don't you think politics play a role in developing the fundamentalists' hatred of us?"

"That's a good point," said George. "At one time the Islamic empire expanded through military campaigns throughout the Middle East, Persia, North Africa and Spain."

The Moors had conquered Spain in the year 711, and the Mediterranean empire that Muslims built flourished in the arts, sciences and mathematics. In Cordoba, Spain, it had especially reached its zenith, and the prosperity was a sign that God was with them. But since the Islamic Empire fell to the invading Mongols around the 13th century, extremists like Bin Laden longed to see the Islamic states and practices rise again. An American military presence made that impossible. In addition, seeing 'infidels' prospering around the world caused resentment, and true believers questioned their own commitment. Their fanaticism increased in diligence and fervor, to be certain they would gain the favor and prosperity of Allah once again.

"And is it true that extremists don't like the United States because of its support for Israel?" asked Randy.

"That's a complicated issue," said George. "At the beginning of the 20th century, Great Britain occupied Palestine. Britain played a significant role in carving the map of the Middle East."

Frustrated with the political consequences of its occupation, Britain turned over the control of Palestine to the United Nations. In 1948, the Security Council voted to partition the land and established the state of Israel. Saudi Arabia's ambassador to the U.N., Prince Faisal, voted against partition. The United States voted in favor of the partition, going back on the promise to consult with Saudi that President Roosevelt had made previously to Faisal's father, King Abdul Aziz. Prince Faisal felt betrayed by the United State's vote in favor of an Israeli state. * He was humiliated and furious. Like most Arabs, he considered the state of Israel a solution to a European problem that arose during WWII. Arab nations refused to recognize Israel as a state, and rioting occurred in Saudi against American citizens working in the eastern province of Dahran. However, Saudi Arabia still needed something from the United States; the military security of the American army.

"Today, most Arabs are outraged by the use of U.S. weapons by the Israeli army but look the other way when Palestinians use Soviet supplied weapons," continued George. "And I don't think Arabs understand how connected Jews feel to the Holy Land. If Islamic scholars read the Old Testament, they might better understand the Jewish yearning for Jerusalem, a land considered home for several millennia."

I added, "In spite of the advances like the Camp David Accords that Jimmy Carter hosted for Egypt and Israel, I guess extremists on both sides disrupt the peace process."

"To the detriment of us all," George said sadly. "But I hope some of this background helps you understand how important our schools are in developing understanding."

George slowed the car down and parked under an acacia tree that sheltered a white stucco wall and building. He said, "There's quite a difference of opinion within the royal family on how to relate to the West and modernize Saudi. But in defense of the royals we work for, the young princes we'll teach have open minds and great character. You'll really like them. They've interacted with the West and they realize they can retain their faith and be modern. They give me hope that we can learn to work together in the future."

The entrance to the school was locked, so George rang a buzzer. An aged little man with humped shoulders slowly opened the large door. His white hair matched his long *thobe* that rippled in the breeze. When he saw George, he pulled the door wide open and shook George's hand fervently.

"*Sabah 'al-hare.* Hallo," shouted the friendly gatekeeper.

""Hello. *Sabah 'al noor.*" said George as he embraced him. George introduced us to Seddar and told him to let us in whenever we arrived.

In the school foyer, a vivid watercolor of an historic desert home with painted wooden doors hung over a blue leather sofa. Healthy ficus trees sprouted from large polished brass pots under the stairs. An Islamic proverb in beautifully scripted Arabic was embroidered with gleaming gold thread upon black fabric. It hung on a wall in the stairwell.

A young Filipino servant appeared and greeted George. "Mr. Phelps, you come back!"

"We love Saudi Arabia, Taylor." Taylor bowed respectfully as George introduced us. George told Taylor to direct Abdullah our way when he came. Apparently, only servants arrived on time, so Abdullah typically arrived late.

Randy asked, "So, we're kinda like servants too?"

"In some respects, I guess so," George admitted, as he led us down a hallway toward the teachers' office.

The office contained seven desks to accommodate all of the teachers. Randy and I were responsible for teaching math, English, social studies and science. The elective teachers would teach art, Spanish, piano, guitar and physical education. An oval table stood near a sliding glass door and opened onto a garden. The grassy yard and sleepy palms provided a calm atmosphere conducive to planning creative lessons.

We were wondering which desks to use when we heard someone walking down the corridor. "Mr. Al-Rasheed! Gosh, it's great to see a familiar face," said Randy, extending his hand.

"Welcome to Saudi Arabia, Mr. Decker, and Mrs. Decker," he said smiling.

Mr. Al-Rasheed pumped Randy's hand vigorously. "Please, call me Abdullah." Abdullah nodded politely toward me. "And how was your trip, Mrs. Decker?"

"It was fine, just a little rough during the landing."

"Don't worry, our pilots are experts! Now, isn't everything just the way I said it would be?"

"It's much better than we imagined," I said. "Thank you for everything you've done. We really appreciate your help in getting us over here safely."

Abdullah smiled proudly. "You see. No one has ever caught me in a lie!"

"We can't wait for school to start," I said.

"Then let me show you around," said Abdullah. "I thought Randy could move into a separate office. Let's look it over."

We followed Abdullah to a small office. Several degrees were nicely displayed on the walls. Professional manuals filled the bookshelf and piles of work were left on the desk. Randy shuffled his feet uneasily since it seemed someone was using the office. Abdullah admitted that Princess Noura's personal assistant, Clarise Stillworth, used the office and helped the children like a secretary, but that the school needed a director.

"I just need a large table for planning like the one in the teachers' office," said Randy.

Abdullah told Randy to keep the office in mind and write a proposal explaining what he'd like his role to be at the school. As we left Clarise's office, Randy said he'd give it some thought. I was delighted because I knew he would make a great administrator. I also would feel secure with him in charge. Surely Clarise could fulfill her secretarial duties in another office.

We followed Abdullah upstairs to the classrooms. I hoped the rooms would help me better understand my new students and give me a sense of what each one was like. The rooms had stark white walls, but Prince Majid's room had blue curtains and accents. The *Qur'an* lay on the top of his worktable; his prayer rug was rolled up and stored upon a tabletop. On the opposite wall was a poster of the Saudi soccer team. A small palm rested quietly in a corner; an acacia tree towered outside the window. Princess Samira's room was done in quiet shades of pink. Papers written in Arabic were scattered about her tabletop. Her notebook and *Qur'an* were left on her desk. A large oil painting with pink, gray and indigo abstract designs covered a white wall.

We were impressed with the facilities throughout the school. As we walked into the reading room, I was glad to see so many English and American classics, history books, reference sources and study guides lining the bookcase shelves. The computer and science labs were state-of-the-art. Downstairs, the music room had a piano, a guitar and several music stands. An art room was filled with acrylic paints, brushes and blank canvases. An artist's easel stood in the corner holding an unfinished watercolor.

The only unimpressive items were the tacky looking posters and school papers left from the previous year. They hung in disarray on the bulletin boards. We'd have to clear the clutter. Our students deserved attractive boards that would motivate them to take pride in their work.

We finished our tour by climbing to the rooftop. Surveying the modern cityscape below was inspiring and helped cement our sense of divine purpose in working at the school. Abdullah told us that the prince and princess wanted to meet us soon. He'd make the arrangements and inform us of the day and time.

Once Abdullah left, we started home. The noon call to prayer rang out from loudspeakers in minarets everywhere. A white Toyota pick-up pulled up beside us with several stern looking men inside. The men wore white prayer caps and had long beards. They sat soberly in the front seat looking in all directions around them.

"The morality squads," explained George. "Just like the ones we saw at the mall. They drive around looking for people not attending prayer. I was standing beside a Pakistani Muslim one day. When I noticed him trying to hide from the *mutawwa,* he said that since he wasn't attending prayer, he could be beaten and deported if they spotted him."

Men clad in their long white thobes streamed along the sidewalks and crossed the roadway toward a mosque at the upcoming intersection.

George stopped at the red light. "Are you getting used to the calls to prayer?"

"Yes, except that first one when we're still asleep," I said.

The light turned green and several cars behind us honked their horns wildly. George glanced in his rearview mirror and sped through the intersection. "Sometimes the prayer is recorded. You should have been here when a teenager switched the prayer tape for a rap tape," said George. "Rap was blasted throughout the neighborhood instead of prayer."

"I guess kids are the same everywhere," Randy said laughing.

"It was clever, but he got in plenty of trouble with the clerics and his family," said George.

Randy's tone turned suddenly serious, and he asked George what he thought about moving into Clarise's office. Both men were uncomfortable about Abdullah's suggested move.

Confident about Randy's leadership qualities I said, "You'd be a great director!"

"But Clarise might be more important than Abdullah thinks. You're not concerned about a woman in charge, are you?" he challenged.

"Oh, please," I retorted, embarrassed by his implications.

"Well, I like teamwork better anyway, and I've been mulling over another idea. The school needs credibility when the children apply for college. If we could connect with a university this year, we'd improve the quality of the school."

Randy outlined his idea for establishing a liaison with a prominent university so educational professors could monitor our school's growth, staff and curriculum. He thought that if they could evaluate our program, they might be able to recommend the children when they applied for college admission. George encouraged Randy to look into it further.

Later that evening, Randy and I met our new American friends for dinner at the compound's restaurant. We strolled along the streets admiring the adobe textures and arched entries of the single-family homes. The Islamic Moors had ruled Spain for centuries, and I realized that the architecture on the compound reminded me of the Spanish missions established in 17th and 18th century California. Bougainvilleas showered an array of garnet blossoms along villa walls and over wooden arbors that framed carports. Leafy palms swayed in the evening breeze; early stars sparkled on the horizon. We wandered by the pool and its deck, but the noisy splashing of the day had evaporated and left the pool area a quiet and restful sanctuary. No wonder Arabian nights were legendary.

We saw George, Lydia, Mike and Jan sitting at a poolside table. George motioned for us to join them. A floral tablecloth with ivory gardenias and jade leaves fell around the corners of the table, complementing a set of white china and crystal wine glasses. In the center, white mums and daisies stood in a brass vase. Nearby, a green marble fountain gurgled softly. I thanked God for leading us to such a beautiful and restful place.

A waiter pulled our chairs out. "We supply wine glasses, but you must bring your own wine."

Randy looked puzzled. "I thought alcohol was illegal."

George smiled and held up two large plastic bottles. "I made a fresh batch of red and white wine. I'll show you how to make it. Around here, we call it 'tea.'"

Randy and Mike chuckled as we handed our crystal glasses to George.

"You can live a fairly normal life in private," said Lydia. "There isn't any public entertainment, but we have satellite television, movies, dance halls, wine and even Bible studies."

"Bible studies?" I asked.

"Sure. We attend one every week at a home of a friend. We have to be discreet, though. A British priest is being kept under house arrest for holding prayer services and possessing Bibles."

"So other faiths aren't tolerated?" asked Randy.

"Not in practice. Mohammed allowed churches and synagogues to exist, but Jews and Christians didn't have equal representation before the law. In early Baghdad, Jews were forced to wear a yellow badge for the purpose of identification," explained George.

The thought of wearing a yellow badge sent shivers down my spine.

"What about women's rights and athletics?" I asked.

"I was wondering about that too," said Jan. "I was skimming a beautiful glossy brochure about all the modern sports facilities in Saudi Arabia when I realized there weren't any women in the pictures. The brochure presented this fantasy world of opportunity, but it was all for men."

"That's true," said Lydia. "Our students said we'd get used to it. Apparently sports are thought to be bad for women."

"I was wondering if there was an ice rink in Riyadh?" I asked, since skating was something I enjoyed on the weekends.

George nodded, "Our neighbors take their boys to a rink nearby to practice hockey, but," he paused, "they said women aren't allowed. Apparently they used to be, but after some kind of problem, the women were kicked out."

I shook my head with disappointment.

While reading the menu, a compound resident approached George and struck up a conversation. George introduced him as a well-known British surgeon and said, "The Deckers and the Barkers will be working for Prince Faisal and his brother-in-law in the private schools they set up for their children."

The doctor frowned. "I hope you get paid. My nurses haven't been paid in months."

"Why don't they just quit?" Randy asked innocently.

The doctor's frown turned into a smirk. "Saudi sponsors hold our passports and return tickets home. Whoever holds the papers holds the power, so we won't do anything to make our sponsor look bad."

I was surprised by the doctor's sense of victimization. He was an educated man.

"And how could asking for your salary make anyone look bad?" Jan challenged.

The surgeon grimaced in mockery, "A Saudi never makes a mistake, so don't back a Saudi into a corner. An old Arabian proverb says that to make a mistake is only the first sin. To admit it is the second. You'd better learn that fast!"

George interrupted the tense discourse, saying, "Our prince always pays his bills."

Mike said, "I'd sure like to get my reimbursements for travel expenses. And I don't like having to turn over my passport to Abdullah."

"We'll talk to Abdullah tomorrow if you'd like," said George.

"Well, good luck," the doctor continued. "Personally, I can't wait for my contract to expire so I can leave this gilded cage." He stared at Randy a moment. "Make sure you're on the right side of the fence, young man!" The doctor turned abruptly and shook his head as he walked away.

Randy frowned. "Geez, what does he mean, 'The right side of the fence?'"

George said that he had heard negative talk like that before. He considered the doctor's gossip insensitive toward the host culture and had determined not to give into that dark and bigoted side. He was sure the doctor was full of arrogance and prejudice and had done something to irritate his Saudi sponsor. Lydia nodded in agreement. Randy and I had worked cross-culturally for years and knew that respect went a long ways, so I pushed the uncertainties out of my mind with hopeful dreams for the future.

George held up his glass. "Here's to your success in your new jobs."

"And to a positive attitude," I said, stifling a yawn. A warm evening breeze drifted across the pool, bringing with it a sweet sedating fragrance.

"Can you smell the jasmine?" asked Lydia.

Jan slowly sipped her wine. "It's lovely, but I can hardly keep my eyes open."

"You're still dealing with jet lag," said Lydia.

"Or I'm becoming numb to my surroundings," Jan said half jokingly.

Mike put his arm around Jan. "Forget that cynical doctor. I'll take care of us."

"You'd better because I was thinking this is a good time to start a family."

Mike winked lovingly at her. He squeezed her so tightly she began laughing and giggling.

"A family?" asked George. "That deserves a toast."

George led us in a toast for the hopeful couple as a soothing breeze enveloped us. The wine relaxed us and the smiles of new friends with dreams for the future filled our hearts with happiness. The chance to make an impact in a changing part of the world was challenging and exciting. We were also grateful that the prince and princess had provided us with such lovely and secure accommodations where we could carry on our lives quite normally and ignore the world outside of its walls.

"Randy, do you forgive me for dragging you half way around the world?" I asked.

"I'd rather have an adventure any day. Besides, we know God is always with us."

As Randy and I tilted our glasses toward each other with a sense of contentment, I felt like we had arrived in Paradise.

5.

WE ARE MUSLIM

RANDY AND I were honored to be working for the royal family and studied the complicated genealogies with fascination. We wondered where our students belonged in the distinguished lineage of rulers. While there were thousands of princes and princesses, the branch of the family we would be working for was the powerful line of brothers often referred to by outsiders as the *Sudeiri Seven*. These brothers were descendants of the first king, Abdul Aziz, and the favorite wife of his youth, Hassa bint Ahmad al-Sudeiri.

During his campaign to establish the kingdom, Abdul Aziz had received ardent and loyal support from his friend Ahmad Al-Sudeiri. Ahmad had a delightful and beautiful young daughter named Hassa. When Abdul Aziz first laid eyes upon her, he was smitten. Since she was a child at the time, he vowed to wait for her to mature. When she turned thirteen he married her. Though once divorced from Aziz, Hassa remarried him and remained his faithful wife. She bore him seven sons and five daughters. She insisted that her family have lunch together daily, and strong bonds were formed among the young men. Within the circle of royals, the seven wielded significant influence. *

The sons of Abdul Aziz and Hassa were among those who assisted Prince Faisal when he ascended the throne after his brother, King Saud. Abdul Aziz had appointed his eldest son to be king as he was dying in 1953. He cautioned his sons, Saud and Faisal, to remain loyal to one another and not let the kingdom become divided. Unfortunately, Saud proved himself to be an ostentatious and corrupt king with little concern for the country, its finances or its citizens. While enjoying the lavish lifestyle of royalty, he either ignored his duties or consistently delegated them to other princes. The brothers became so concerned about the state of the country that they met to determine what should be done. After much discussion, they obtained a religious ruling known as a *fatwa* from the *ulema,* or religious leaders. Together, the princes deposed King Saud and exiled him to Athens, Greece. The family replaced Saud with his younger brother, Crown Prince Faisal.*

Hassa bint Sudeiri was also the mother of King Fahad. Fahad's first wife had fallen gravely ill with kidney disease, so he married a second wife. In 1995, King Fahad became ill himself and suffered a serious stroke. Crown Prince Abdullah, a half brother to Fahad, assumed the duties of king, but not the title. Hassa's other sons held prominent positions in government as well. * Prince Sultan was the Minister of Defense and Prince Turki was Sultan's assistant for several years. Another son, Prince Salman, was the influential Governor of Riyadh and hoped to become king. Prince Salman had married a beautiful and generous woman named Sultana. She distinguished herself as one of the kindest and most caring women in the kingdom and was frequently sought out by other women for comfort and advice. Though often ill, Sultana bore Prince Salman several sons. One of them, Prince Ahmed, spent much of his time at world-renowned racetracks. Another son, Sultan, distinguished himself as the first astronaut in Saudi Arabia. Her sons grew to bring her honor among the family. Many in Riyadh considered the intelligent and conservative Salman a favorite candidate for the throne. Because of his background, Majid also had the potential to ascend the throne. As a result, Randy and I took our responsibility to help prepare future leaders most seriously.

Several days after our dinner on the compound, Abdullah called and said that arrangements had been made for us to meet Prince Faisal and his wife, Princess Noura. The personal assistant to Princess Noura, Clarise Stillworth, called as well. She reassured us that the prince and princess we worked for were down-to-earth. They were modern and accustomed to interacting with Americans. We wanted to show respect toward Islam, so we dressed conservatively and agreed to let Randy do most of the talking. During the meeting, we would be introduced to the princess' unique vision for the future of Saudi Arabia and encounter some unexpected and intriguing palace politics.

Randy drove anxiously toward the palace district. Like the ones surrounding his, Prince Faisal's palace was a block long and was surrounded by thick stucco walls a story high. Randy and I had been instructed to use the family gate where only women and children were allowed. Due to the separation of the genders, men used an entrance on the other side of the palace. When we told the security guard that we were the new teachers, he pushed a button. The massive wooden gate swung open slowly. Through the soft light that flowed from wrought iron lampposts, we could see the expansive palace grounds. The marble palace was three stories high. Arched windows trimmed with white marble stretched gracefully across the front. The ruddy tiled roof curved slightly skyward. Towering date palms reached over the top of the roof and sheltered immense flower gardens below.

We walked up the steps of the main residence and waited at a stained glass door. A young Filipina maid opened it for us. An enormous crystal chandelier hung over a round mahogany table in the center of the foyer. An arrangement of several dozen pink roses in a luminous crystal vase adorned the table. A blue Persian rug covered the ivory marble floors. Ficus plants in a shiny brass pots stood in every corner.

The maid directed us into a waiting room. The sofas were covered with a beautiful tapestry that had a beige background with an array of floral patterns in hues of blue, purple, pink and jade. They were strewn with beige silk pillows that were embroidered with colorful flowers. Silk drapes plummeted from the high ceiling to the floor and matched the sofas. The drapes were tied back at the center with a silk tassel and ivory sheers billowed out between them. The beige Chinese carpet had a wide pink border; the center medallion was created with pink flowers and jade leaves. Hanging in the middle of the room was a jade chandelier. At one end of the carpet were two ivory velvet chairs with an antique Chinese table in between. A large painting of Arabian warriors riding majestic horses across desert sands was set in an ornate gilded frame. Princess Noura's palace was as glorious as I had imagined it would be. I learned later that she and her husband had chosen the decorations themselves.

Another maid entered with a silver tray and offered us fruit drinks in crystal water goblets. I took one gingerly and set it on a glass inset of the mahogany coffee table. It was covered with a dozen silver nick knacks: lighters, figurines, ashtrays, and a variety of decorative flower vases. Each end table had a large vase of fresh flowers. Candy and cookies filled silver bowls but I was too tense to sample any.

A sophisticated young woman with wavy brown hair and dark creamy skin entered the room and introduced herself as Clarise Stillworth. She was from England, and had worked for Princess Noura for three years. Clarise addressed us. "The princess will be with us momentarily. How is everything so far?"

"Great. Abdullah showed us around the school a few days ago," said Randy. "He's done a lot to help us settle in and get comfortable."

"Speaking of Abdullah, here he comes," said Clarise. Nodding a stiff welcome, she said, "Good afternoon. The prince and princess will be here shortly. Please, have a seat."

Abdullah shook our hands, took a nearby seat and pulled a legal pad out of his briefcase. Clarise sat across the room. Randy straightened his tie. I'd become so nervous I thought I could throw up. I silently pleaded with God to calm my nerves and help me make a good impression.

At last, a poised and stunning woman in her late thirties with dark brown hair and kind eyes entered. She wore an ankle length denim dress that was gathered and tucked with thick brown thread over the bodice. Her brown suede pumps complemented the trim. The confidence and dignity of her carriage told us immediately who she was before she even uttered a word. Everyone stood. The princess smiled and extended her hand toward me.

"Hello, I am Noura." A gold watch with about thirty karats of brilliant diamonds and sapphires adorned her delicate wrist.

I extended my hand, though no diamond studded watch slid down my wrist. It seemed natural to dip into a curtsy. This must have been acceptable, for she went about greeting my husband as if nothing unusual happened.

Though regal and elegant, she wasn't anything like the visible and stuffy European royals I had seen on television. Her smile and warmth put me at ease. The princess gestured toward the sofas and told us to be seated. She politely inquired about our flight and the comfort of our villa. Abdullah addressed Her Highness in Arabic and prepared to take notes.

Two young teenagers strode into the room. Proudly the princess said, "My son, Majid, and daughter, Samira." Once again, we rose. Prince Majid shook our hands and took a seat across from Randy. Though Majid was extremely polite, he had an impish smile with eyes that sparkled like his mother's. He wore blue jeans and a white Manchester United soccer jersey. Princess Samira greeted us and sat beside her mother. She was slight of stature and had fine features. Thick dark lashes framed her coffee brown eyes and her shiny hair fell gracefully around her shoulders. She wore tan jeans with a white blouse and white platform sandals.

"Are you our new teachers?" asked the young prince.

Randy and I nodded politely. "Yes, and we're very honored to be," said Randy.

Princess Samira fidgeted in her chair. "Are you going to give us a test today?"

When I said we'd do that when school started, both teens looked greatly relieved. Princess Noura gave Majid an encouraging nod and he assumed the role of host. He went to great lengths discussing his favorite subject, astronomy. Because he spoke so rapidly, I figured that he, too, must be a little nervous. I couldn't help but like him. Suddenly, Majid jumped up from his seat.

"*Baba!*" he shouted.

A tall, dignified man in a white *thobe* and solid white *ghutra* entered the room. Princess Noura rose from her chair, so we did as well. The prince smiled and extended his hand. "Mr. and Mrs. Decker, I presume. I am Faisal. Delighted to meet you."

Randy grasped the prince's hand firmly. "And we're delighted to meet you, Your Highness."

I shook the prince's hand saying, "It's an honor, Your Highness."

"Please, be seated," said Prince Faisal as he sat beside the princess. "So, onto business. It appears you will be educating my children."

Randy said, "And we're most pleased to do so, Your Highness."

The prince asked, "Have you been to Saudi Arabia before?"

"No," said Randy, "but Kristin's brother and his wife lived in Riyadh for three years."

The prince spoke with a disarming smile. "Then you know that we are often perceived as a bit strict, but if your manner and attire here today are any indication, you will have no trouble. We appreciate your sensitivity to our ways." The prince leaned forward. "You have heard about the dreadful bombing at the army barracks in Dhahran?"

"Yes," said Randy. "When it hit the news, Abdullah called to reassure us."

"Very unfortunate business. But I assure you that you will be safer in our city than on the streets of New York or Chicago."

"Or Los Angeles," I added, thinking of where I had taught during the fierce and terrifying riots in South Central following the announcement of the verdict in the trial of the officers beating Rodney King.

The prince nodded. "Yes. And you should know I travel frequently on business, so I am not here as much as I would like to supervise the education of my children. I have committed the task to the very capable hands of my wife. You will be directly responsible to her, so I will leave you with her now. She can fill you in on the details of the education we want for our children. We are interested in having them attend prominent Western schools in either England or America." He stood, so we did, as did the princess. "Oh, everything is fine with your villa, I trust?"

"It's wonderful," said Randy. "And we appreciate everything Mr.

Al-Rasheed has done."

Suddenly, everyone in the room became silent and stared at Abdullah. He took a deep breath and nodded respectfully in our direction.

Finally the prince smiled and said that he would see us around. He shook our hands and left.

"Well, on to the children's education," the princess began. "I should let you know that in our schools everything is memorize, memorize, memorize. Facts, facts, facts. It is not enough. I want my children to learn how to think! I do not want their education with you to be more and more facts stuffed into their heads. I want them to enjoy learning. I want your focus in each subject to be on the crème de la crème so that they can have a broad understanding of each subject. I want them to converse intelligently wherever they go and with whomever they are around."

I was glad George had prepared us with background information for it made it easy to understand and support the princess. She had an admirable vision for her children and country that revealed her intelligence and diplomacy. I considered her a wise woman.

"And you must understand we are Muslim," continued the princess. "I want them exposed to different ideas, but I do not want our values questioned. There are things in our country that are not as they should be. We know that. We are well aware of what needs to change. But we also know change takes time. We do not want to create instability in our people because we change too fast. We ask that in your teaching you respect this process. Am I making sense? Please, tell me what you think."

I explained to Her Highness that people from all over the world lived in California, and that we had taught students from many countries with a variety of values. We thought the differences were enriching and assured her that we would teach with the same respect in her country.

She looked relieved and then glanced toward Clarise. "Clarise has an office at the school. I want her to be head director, especially until you are more familiar with school operations."

I heard Abdullah shuffling his feet in the background, but the children smiled. Clarise wanted to take Randy and me out to lunch to discuss the school's history and the children's progress. Randy politely offered drive us anywhere she liked. While she smiled, something in her eyes made her seem distant. The princess asked Clarise to call her every day and apprise her of the children's progress. Finally, Princess Noura rose to shake our hands.

Randy and I spoke briefly with Majid and Samira and then met with Abdullah outside. He was dumbfounded over Clarise's appointment and couldn't understand why the princess had acted without consulting him first. Apparently embarrassed by her independent action, Abdullah explained that he answered to Prince Faisal anyway. He advised Randy to go ahead and submit the proposal about being head director and then quickly excused himself.

As Randy and I got into our car, Clarise approached us. "I want you to know something. *I* will be taking *you* out to lunch. An ace beats a king, beats a queen, beats a jack. I'm here on behalf of Prince Faisal. You're here on behalf of Princess Noura. So, shall we meet for coffee at the Intercontinental Hotel tomorrow at 2:00 p.m.?"

"That'll be fine," replied Randy as he started the car.

"Have a nice evening." Clarise turned abruptly away.

I watched her walk toward the gardens. "Oh, my God. What have we walked into?"

"I just want to teach the kids," said Randy.

We were relieved he hadn't moved into Clarise's office, and though we didn't want to insult Abdullah by refusing to submit his proposal, we ultimately answered to the princess and would support her decisions. For the children's sake, we hoped we could move the school forward without insulting anyone. At least the prince had thanked us for our sensitivity to Islamic ways and thought we would do well.

The following day we met Clarise downtown. Once we were seated in the restaurant, Clarise pulled her scarf off and threw it carelessly around her neck. I was surprised by her bold public act. Sensing my confusion, she explained that the *mutawwa* had been told not to patrol hotels rigidly because of the international clientele. The children's grandfather was the one who implemented the ruling. Immediately she focused on business, her curt manner making clear that she wasn't interested in befriending us. "The princess wants you to know exactly what you're getting into, so she told me to paint the picture as black as I could."

"I'm confident about working with the children one at a time," Randy replied.

"My family has a long history of educating royalty, and there are things you need to understand. Teachers who've worked with only middle-class students can be in for a rough time. It seems that the very wealthy, as well as the very poor, live by their own set of standards and have their own rules. They have a different view of the world. They're motivated differently. Teachers need to be flexible."

Clarise pulled our resumes out of a file. "Where was your previous teaching experience?"

"South Central Los Angeles," I replied.

"Watts," answered Randy.

She paused briefly and said, "Oh."

"So, the poor and the wealthy have a lot in common?" asked Randy.

Clarise explained that since Majid and Samira would not have to grow up and hold down a job, working hard to go to college and get a job wouldn't necessarily motivate them. Majid's parents and teachers agreed that he was very intelligent. In spite of that, he was having a hard time keeping up with a program based on rote memorization. One time he couldn't finish a writing assignment and his teacher called him a donkey. Majid was furious and stormed out of the room. He marched down the hall, short circuited the electrical power and called his father who was out of the country on business.

Rather than being discouraged, I was challenged. "Majid must not have a traditional style of learning. Besides, shame isn't a good motivator for any student."

"This is a shame and honor based society. What can you do?" asked Clarise.

Randy said, "We must find his style of learning and build his confidence."

"The princess believes he can be reached if the right buttons are pushed," said Clarise.

I wondered how the princess knew so much about education. Clarise said she was very well read and that her family was highly educated. They had attended the best universities in America and realized that Western schools teach students *how to think* without telling them *what to think*. The prince and princess believed the children could get a modern education and retain their faith.

Clarise studied our resumes again. "The princess would like the children to learn about the stock market. Are you qualified to teach about stocks?"

I tried to ignore the challenging tone of her voice and begged God to grant me patience and understanding. Fortunately, Randy answered calmly. "I have a broker's license and have worked part-time for a brokerage firm for five years."

"And I use the stock market to teach math," I added somewhat smugly.

"This is good news indeed!" Clarise stared at our resumes for a few more moments. "You do understand that the children will grow up to be important leaders of their country?"

"That's why we accepted this position," I said, feeling like I was being interviewed for a second time. I wondered who was really in charge. Was it Abdullah or Clarise?

Randy added, "Talking everything over with you makes me feel like I've been preparing for this position for the last ten years. We've had experience teaching cross culturally, we've worked with different economic groups and we can teach intelligently about the stock market from firsthand experience. It's as if providence led us here . . . almost like a calling of some kind."

I nodded in agreement with my husband, for we felt we had the right experience and the doors had opened easily and smoothly.

"Your background experience in Los Angeles certainly will be an asset." She took a deep breath. "Well, maybe this will work out after all."

Clarise offered to help with any discipline issues that arose and promised to call the children's mother if necessary. Randy explained that in Los Angeles schools we'd handled chairs flying across the rooms, tables being turned over, defiance, accusations of racism, riots, disgruntled parents, and baseball bats used in class fights, and without much support from administrators. He knew we could handle a prince and a princess, especially one at a time.

Randy thanked Clarise politely, but his deference annoyed me. I still wasn't sure Clarise was qualified to be in charge of a school program. I'd seen unqualified people in positions of authority ruin private schools. "By the way," I said, "Where did you get your credentials in education?"

"I went to Oxford. My bachelor's is in English literature and my master's is in business administration."

Suddenly Clarise glanced around the restaurant. Two businessmen in Western attire were present, but they were sitting across the room. She leaned over the table and whispered, "Do not discuss this school with anyone. The prince and princess are committed to providing their children with the most comprehensive education possible, but not everyone in their extended family supports their decision. The royals have a long history of providing education *par excellence* for their children with private schools, and today there are a number of schools like ours, but they're actually frowned upon by the conservatives."

Randy asked, "Is this going to be a problem?"

"Not if we're quiet. This school is Princess Noura's dream. Her own father, who lives in London, supports her. He's the one who pays our salaries, but Noura's father-in-law closed it down last year when he learned about it. The father-in-law hopes to become king one day and is worried about offending the conservatives and clerics. Noura would be devastated if anything happened to it again."

"How could anyone object to a school like this?" asked Randy.

"Like Noura said, the Saudi schools focus primarily on rote memorization. I also suspect they teach with an anti-Western bias. Noura's school swims against the stream, as have many before hers."

Even though previous royals and rulers had promoted a broader educational approach within the context of extending Islamic values, clerics often objected to the inclusion of the sciences and languages. The tension had been in place since King Saud first tried to improve education, including education for women. *

"So even within the royal family there is disagreement about how to move the country forward?" I asked.

"Oh, yes. No matter how much of a united front they present to the rest of the world, there are reports of heated, often violent, clashes among them. They are very passionate."

"We won't say anything," I said with a growing respect for the princess. "We don't know anyone to talk to anyway."

"The princess would eventually like to come to the school for English lessons," said Clarise. "It would only be appropriate for a woman to teach her."

"I'd love to tutor her," I said. "Perhaps she'd like to read one of Jane Austen's books, like *Pride and Prejudice.* Are English classics available in Saudi?"

"The better bookstores carry a number of English language classics. I'm sure you could find one of the Austen novels. Perhaps you could also look for a Bronte novel. Noura might enjoy reading about an English heroine who takes charge of her life and refuses to be controlled by her culture."

Princess Noura reminded me of the strong and spirited protagonists of many English novels, who pursued their dreams in spite of their culture's limitations. As a result, they discovered authentic and caring relationships in a world often consumed with outward appearances and financial gain.

Clarise smiled, rose and stretched out her hand. "Welcome aboard."

When I stood, I knocked over my coffee cup, splattering coffee all over Clarise and her files. Randy rushed to help wipe off the files. Clarise searched desperately for napkins.

"I am so sorry," I muttered. I knew my cheeks were turning red with embarrassment.

Clarise grabbed a napkin and brushed the coffee off of her *abaya* and papers. With tightly pursed lips she said, "I'll see you at school on Saturday. Be early, so I can go over the schedule."

Randy nodded stiffly. Clarise grabbed her bag and marched out of the restaurant. I saw her snap her fingers at Akbar who was waiting patiently in the hotel lobby. He followed her obediently out of the hotel.

Randy asked, "How could you be so clumsy? She was just warming up to us."

"It was an accident," I said, brushing the coffee from my *abaya*. "I felt patronized by her. Abdullah never implies I'm incompetent. Maybe she's well educated, but what does she know about teaching, let alone administering a school program?"

"She knows what the princess wants, and we're an ideal fit for the school. I always wondered why I ended up teaching after seminary, but that prepared us for this job. We have experience in everything they need. We can't let politics interfere with the vision of the school. Clarise will relax once she sees how well we work with kids. Besides, I think you're a better teacher than I am."

Since I felt like my professionalism had been challenged, I didn't realize how much I needed support until he complimented me. I respected the prince and princess and their vision for their children to be educated and diplomatic so they could lead their country forward without causing instability, but I was not looking forward to working with the only other Westerner on staff.

6.

A PATH TO SUCCESS

IT WAS SATURDAY, the first day of the Saudi work week and the opening day of school. Randy and I began the morning with our regular devotions, prayer time and cups of freshly brewed coffee. We asked God for his help and wisdom. We prayed that he lead us along paths of righteousness so our lives would honor his name. Around ten a.m. we drove to the school for an early meeting with Clarise.

Once settled, she handed us the children's schedules and reiterated the need for appropriate discipline and motivation. When Randy suggested that the children outline their own personal goals and create a banner to illustrate them, Clarise seemed modestly pleased. We agreed that if our students were properly motivated, discipline would naturally follow and we'd be able to keep moving forward with the curriculum.

When the meeting was over, I marched upstairs to finish preparing. From the class window I saw a black Chevy Suburban park in front. Majid jumped out of the passenger side, his long thobe rippling in the breeze. His tiny Filipina nanny exited the back door with his soccer clothes. Majid's driver picked up his backpack and followed him through the gate. The driver greeted Seddar, the gatekeeper whom we had met on our first visit. Within minutes, a dark blue Suburban parked behind Majid's. Draped in black, Samira got out of the back. Her nanny, also completely covered, followed her into the school. The children's drivers exchanged greetings. Each one lit up a cigarette and entered a small waiting room where Seddar usually watched television until the children called upon him.

I hurried downstairs to greet the children. Clarise was still in her office, so Randy and I entered the kitchen. Majid and Samira greeted us respectfully. Samira's nanny, Cora, introduced herself. She was a pleasant woman of middle age and made us feel welcomed. She offered to help us should we ever need it. Next we introduced ourselves to the new art teacher, Zoe, and sat beside her. Zoe had grown up in New Zealand and met her husband while attending university in Canada. They had lived in the kingdom for the last five years and she had just started working for Princess Noura. Her husband worked for a high tech company and she had two darling boys. When she explained that she knew George and Lydia, we realized we were neighbors. Her cheerful and positive disposition made me anxious to befriend her.

The Spanish teacher, Luis, had yet to arrive. We sat quietly, wondering what to do next. When Abdullah arrived, we breathed a collective sigh of relief. He greeted everyone and politely carried the conversation, asking the children about their lessons earlier in the morning at the public schools.

Clarise entered and directed everyone to follow her to the large office for the opening meeting. I noticed Abdullah stiffen at the order, and I bristled at her curt demeanor. But we followed her anyway and sat around the oval table where she had displayed the school rules and schedule. Abdullah sat at the head of the table. The Spanish teacher arrived and excused himself for being late. The music and computer teachers planned to come every other day and were not present. The physical education teachers would meet the children later in the palace gardens.

As Clarise opened the meeting, I realized that Princess Noura held the children to high standards. Majid and Samira were expected to follow school rules like any other student. The young prince and princess also carried a heavy load of academic classes. At their grandfather's insistence, they spent all morning in a Saudi public school. In the afternoon, they studied the American curriculum at our school, paid for by their other grandfather. Though the children had a rigorous schedule, I realized that Majid and Samira would emerge as diplomats both at home and abroad when they were old enough. They were being enriched by both cultures.

Clarise explained the goal setting project and dismissed the children. She gathered her papers and dismantled the display. Zoe and Luis excused themselves and walked toward their desks.

Abdullah addressed Randy. "This is a great start. We have the right people this year."

"We appreciate your support," Randy said.

When Clarise left the room, Abdullah lowered his voice. "Keep your eye on the spending. The princess and I think Clarise spends too much money."

Since I had felt patronized by her, I was pleased about keeping an eye on her and agreed to do so.

Abdullah said, "And Randy, I'd like to see your role expanded."

Randy shifted his weight uneasily. "I'm giving it some thought."

Abdullah nodded and left the school. The proposal kept coming up, and I was relieved, knowing that I'd feel more secure with a professional in charge. Randy simply wanted to focus on the kids, believing Clarise was more important than Abdullah gave her credit for. Though annoyed with Randy's shortsightedness, I needed to focus on the task before me and prayed, *Dear Lord, please give me the strength and patience for what lies ahead of me today. Help me care for the children with your heart.*

Samira was waiting politely in the classroom. I hoped the goal planning session would give me a chance to know her better and asked her to tell me about the things she enjoyed doing.

She thought for a moment. "I love to paint, and I buy a lot of paintings, especially when we travel. I also like animals."

"So you're an artist! What do you plan to do when you grow up?"

"I want to get married and have lots of kids, of course. But I like school and want to get a good education. Maybe I'll become a doctor or a university professor. I've always wanted to do something important with my life and help people."

Knowing she was at the age when dreams begin to speak to our hearts and unfold before us, I said, "You're in a position where you can do a lot of good. Dream big, and expect miracles."

Though her eyes softened she said, "Well, things are different here." She divided the large poster board into several sections. As she sketched a picture of a mother and child, she asked if I had any children.

"No," I answered, "and if I did have children, I wouldn't be here teaching you today. This position advertised for a couple without children." Though I'd always expected us to have a family, I decided there must have been a providential reason I never experienced an overwhelming desire to have my own children.

She smiled. "I'm glad to have so many cousins and aunts. We do everything together. Won't you feel alone when you're older?"

"Mr. Decker is my best friend. We'll grow old together, and we have two dogs."

She looked up and asked, "You have dogs?"

"Yes, and since no one would look after them like we do, we asked Abdullah if we could bring them."

"Abdullah," she muttered under her breath with apparent disgust.

"I'm glad our dogs could come with us." I felt a little defensive and hoped that the family didn't consider our dogs an insult. I knew dogs were frequently considered unclean. When she mentioned that she had a pet bunny, I was relieved.

Shadowy, ghost-like figures behind dark lines slowly emerged on her poster. Samira explained that they represented Saudi women in their *abayas*. The dark lines represented prison bars that kept women oppressed. Samira wanted to do something to change their plight and explained how many of the women in her family had worked diligently to improve life for women inside the kingdom.

Iffat Al-Thunayan was a close friend of Hassa bint Sudeiri. Iffat, a lovely woman with fair skin and auburn hair, was the wife of the third king, Faisal. She was an indomitable woman and became known as a leading force for progress in the kingdom. * It was she who implemented education for women during the 1940s. Initially, she opened small private schools for her children and those of like-minded families. When the first public school for girls opened in Buraydah, a town north of Riyadh, violence erupted. King Faisal sent in the National Guard to keep the school open. In time, Iffat convinced leading *imams* that educated women were better mothers and that spiritual training should start in the home. An educated mother was better for Islam. Her husband, King Faisal, lent his support by pointing out that the *Qur'an* did not forbid the education of women. Iffat later established a training college for women to become teachers. She also worked to see that the curriculum for both boys and girls was broader than the mere memorization of *Qur'anic* verses. She advocated the inclusion of subjects like science and study of foreign languages. * Princess Noura was carrying on the same proud tradition for her children. In light of Iffat's challenges with the religious leaders, I understood why Noura still found it necessary to keep the school private and secret.

After forty-five minutes, Clarise rang the bell. Samira put down her pencil and said, "I'll finish this tomorrow. Zoe is waiting for me in the art room."

Majid entered and sat in the swivel chair. He spun the chair around. "So, what do you teach?"

"English and math."

He made a sour face. "Math, yuck!"

I quickly prayed for the right words. "Oh, I love math. I'll show you some different ways to do it. But today, you need to think of what you'd like to accomplish with your life."

He came to a stop and thought about the question. "I want to be a businessman like my father."

"I guess you'll have to go to college."

"I plan to. My father used to work in government, but other people took credit for his ideas. He likes the people he worked with; he just didn't like the way they did things sometimes."

"It feels unfair when others take credit for your work," I agreed.

Clarise walked slowly by the open door. "Majid, are you spinning in the chair?"

He stopped spinning immediately. "Oh, sorry," he said. The 'spinning chair rule' was somewhat amusing, but I supposed it had been an issue for either Clarise or a previous teacher.

Majid continued. "If I'm a businessman, I can make enough money to build a hospital for the Saudi people. They could get free medical care. And I want to tell kids everywhere not to do drugs. And I want countries to live peacefully together."

I couldn't imagine someone had called this kind-hearted young man a donkey.

"Hey," he said, spinning in his chair. "Did you see my poster of the Saudi soccer team?"

"That's the first thing I noticed in your room. Remember the chair, Majid," I said.

"Oh yeah." He stopped the chair. "I play soccer every night after school." Then he picked up a pencil and began tapping it on the desk. Majid was simultaneously a prince and a young boy enthusiastic about life and sports. He took a whirl in the chair again. "Oh, sorry," he said, eyeing me carefully. He brought his chair to a stand still.

It was time to start his project, so he grabbed a pencil and started drawing. Obviously, Majid meant to comply. I was relieved he was trying to cooperate and respected my authority as his teacher. Forcing him into the traditional style of learning might mean losing him, his bright mind, his jubilant enthusiasm and all of his potential contributions to society. I'd have to incorporate his abundant energy into the learning process with a wide variety of projects and assignments. I was glad I didn't have twenty-nine other students and that I could give Majid all of my attention. Private tutoring was an ideal setting in which he could flourish. As he left he said, "I like your class. You're a nice teacher."

I felt like I had passed a test and thanked the Lord for his help. Majid's response was encouraging, and I prayed it signaled more success for him ahead. I also knew he would keep me on my toes.

When the projects were completed, Clarise framed them and hung them in the classrooms to remind Majid and Samira of what they were working for. I hoped that the goals would inspire them to work hard, stay focused on their lessons and develop a lifelong love for learning.

Randy, Clarise and I met with Zoe and Luis. We designed a unit on ancient Egypt with mock archeological digs in social studies, Egyptian art projects using real papyrus and models of the pyramids to be measured and constructed in math. In English, the children would read a documentary about the excavations of the noted British Egyptologists, Lord Carnarvon and Howard Carter. Since Egypt was a short flight from Riyadh, we planned a field trip to Cairo, Giza and the Valley of the Kings. In the lobby, I tore down the old tacky papers and put up a beautiful navy blue background. I used a metallic blue and gold trim for the border. Randy hung a painting of a Pharaoh done on papyrus. Clarise found a picture of the Sphinx, and for the next six weeks, we immersed ourselves in the study of ancient Egypt as if we too were archaeologists.

As the weeks flew by, classes went smoothly, but lunch transpired into something out of the ordinary. Initially, Majid and Samira sat at a separate table where they were served first. Clarise invited Randy, Zoe and me to have lunch, but we sat at a different table. Before long, we grew weary of yelling back and forth. Finally, the young prince and princess joined the teachers at the larger table. Sometimes lunch became a loud and boisterous affair, but as long as the students were respectful, we were comfortable. Lunch became a welcomed break from the quick pace of our intense academic schedule.

During lunch one afternoon Samira asked, "Mrs. Decker, would you like to see a wedding?"

"A princess' wedding?" I asked. "I've dreamed about going to a royal wedding!"

Majid promptly spoke up. "Mr. Decker, would you like to go to a soccer match with me and my best friend, Ahmed? You could sit in the royal box."

"It'd be cool to see a soccer game," said Randy.

"So, the case is settled," said Majid smiling. "Mr. Decker, you will go to the soccer match with me, and Mrs. Decker you will go to the wedding with Samira."

While Randy and I knew we'd be able to establish mutual respect and witness the children's academic success, their warm and receptive responses were more than we had anticipated. Their consideration and thoughtfulness were better than any paycheck and encouraged us to pursue excellence.

One morning, before the children arrived, Randy and I were drinking a cup of coffee in our office and planning the day's lessons.

We heard someone quickly approaching in the marble hallway. Suddenly Clarise flung open the door and marched in. I caught my breath, unsure whether to smile or brace myself for a confrontation. My mind raced through recent events, wondering if there was some *faux pas* we may have committed.

"I've become accustomed to dealing with conflict in this job," she began. "I'm always in the middle, bearing bad news from the teachers back to the princess." She broke into a smile. "With you two, I've had the pleasure of telling the princess that the children are eating right out of your hands! Neither she nor I have seen the children so anxious to learn, so excited about school and so disciplined. Well done, from the princess and me."

I could hardly believe the compliment I was hearing and did my best to stifle an audible sigh of relief.

"Majid has always been such a rebel about schoolwork. How did you do it?" asked Clarise.

I explained, "Majid has a non-traditional learning style, so we addressed that instead of forcing him into a mold."

"As long as we're passing compliments around, I appreciate the freedom you give us to do our jobs," said Randy.

Clarise laughed. She loved the mutual admiration society that seemed to be emerging. I relaxed a little, but I knew Clarise would always hold the ace. She had the ear of the princess, and if she ever turned on us, well . . . I quickly dismissed the thought.

Clarise sat across from us and explained that we needed to know that Majid's success at our school made his challenges in the public school all the more painfully apparent. He was still struggling and was a constant discipline problem. Some teachers were afraid to correct him because he was a prince, so they left the job to Abdullah.

"Princess Noura said public schools focus primarily on memorization," I said.

Clarise nodded. "Exactly. They push the wrong buttons, and the curriculum isn't like anything we're accustomed to in the West. While there is plenty of instruction in math and writing, there is a strong focus on simply memorizing and rehearsing the *Qur'an*. Most of the royals, however, have been exposed to the world outside of Arabia and understand they can keep their faith and become educated as well."

I wondered if Majid didn't experience some condescension and criticism in the public school setting because of his varied life experiences. He was probably smarter than his teachers. Next, Clarise related her concerns about what could happen when Prince Faisal returned from London. He'd entrusted Abdullah with Majid's public school education and the prince would hold Abdullah responsible. This could be a potential source of embarrassment, so she wanted to take a teamwork approach. If we worked with Majid's Arabic tutors at our school, it could help Abdullah save face.

Since one of the tutors would be a religion teacher, the female teachers at our school would need to keep their a*bayas* on. We didn't want to bring criticism on the family for hiring 'infidels.' Clarise explained that the tension between the clerics and the rulers had started developing with the first king, Abdul-Aziz. And today, while many fundamentalists wanted Westerners thrown out, younger royals understood the need for a thorough education so their children could converse with leaders around the world for the benefit of Saudi Arabia.

Clarise stopped suddenly. I sensed she might have regretted saying too much. Clarise told us not to worry because the prince and princess knew what they wanted and would protect the school.

Randy said, "I appreciate your insights, Clarise. We don't know what we would have done without another Westerner here to show us the ropes. When we first arrived, Abdullah asked me to write a proposal about being school director. It seemed odd because no one should be left out of the process. When I submit the proposal, I'll recommend that the three of us collaborate."

"Thanks, Randy," she said smiling. "That tells me a lot about your character and who you are. Actually, I simply came here to say that the princess and the children want to thank you."

The children wanted to take us to dinner at a Japanese restaurant. If we could drive to the palace that evening, we'd go together in their stretch van. Randy laughed at the thought of a stretch SUV, and I thanked Clarise for their thoughtfulness.

Driving home, Randy said, "Clarise clarified some of the dynamics around us."

"I'm afraid to trust her," I said. "I don't like having so many go-betweens with us and the family. Abdullah is a go-between; Clarise is a go-between . . . who knows what they could say? And now with all of these tutors and a cleric coming, I don't know. What if the cleric sabotages the school because we're teaching the American curriculum?"

"The prince is too smart to let that happen. And a team approach will let us do our problem solving, so everyone has input."

Later that evening Randy and I returned to the palace. Clarise gave us a brief tour of the grounds while we waited for Majid and Samira to get ready. First she escorted us through a huge recreation villa with a billiards table and a home entertainment center. We walked through an immaculate kitchen onto a porch and outdoor BBQ that overlooked the luscious palace gardens and pool. While strolling through the gardens, Samira emerged from a glass building.

Samira invited me into her sitting room to see her bunny. Clarise and Randy headed for the driveway where the stretch van was parked. I followed Samira to a corner of the room where her bunny huddled in a cage. She pulled out the fluffy rabbit and held it close. She let me hold it for a moment. Its warm little body wiggled in my arms.

Clarise finally called us, so we put the rabbit back and headed toward the van. A stranger about Majid's age was standing beside Majid. "Mrs. Decker, this is my best friend, Ahmed. He brought his baseball bats."

I was puzzled and asked, "Are we going to play baseball?"

All three teenagers laughed boisterously at my question.

"Mrs. Decker! It's to hit any guy who harasses my sister," explained Majid.

What surprised me was how matter-of-fact the teens were about it, but I didn't want to sound ignorant, so I said, "Oh, yes, of course."

Their comments made me acutely aware of how dangerous it was for women to venture into the city streets alone. Lydia had mentioned that men had different needs, and the children had presented their solution.

The children jumped into the van and Clarise motioned for Randy and me to step in next. Clarise and the nannies climbed in after us. On the way, the children relaxed and acted like typical teens. Samira had the driver put a CD on and turn the volume up as loud as possible. Our entourage drove through the city streets with Samira singing to the top of her lungs and Majid and Ahmed yelling over Samira. The adults laughed and used gestures to communicate since our attempts to converse were thwarted by the youngsters' noisy antics. When we parked in front of the restaurant, the teens became immediately subdued.

Inside, Majid instructed the host to take us to a private table that was enclosed by a tall screen. At school, Randy and I had become accustomed to telling the young prince what to do and when. But now Majid emerged as the true prince he was and took complete responsibility for everything. The waiter understood that the prince was in charge and took all directions from him. Once the order was placed, the fun and laughter started up again. Though the adults were beginning to tire, the teens' enthusiasm and intent to have a good time energized us.

"We call them Rowdy Saudis," said Clarise.

Samira said, "You should have seen us at Planet Hollywood in London!"

"Yeah! If you think this is loud," said Majid. "We really had a great time there."

"I can imagine," I said, suppressing a yawn. I was glad to see them enjoying themselves since they followed such a rigorous routine at school.

"We want to take you out for Chinese food too," added Majid.

"That's fine with us as long as you ask your mother," said Randy.

"And we'd like to take you some place American like Fuddruckers," I said.

"I love Fuddruckers," said Samira.

"I'll just clear it with your mother," said Clarise.

When the children were ready to leave, Majid arranged for the bill to be paid. He instructed the drivers to take the leftovers home to their families. Outside, several old women surrounded the stretch van. Their faces were wrinkled, puffy and dry, making me think they'd fallen upon hard times. As the children approached the van, the women ran up to them asking something of Majid. We stepped into the van and Majid gave the women some money.

Randy and I thanked the children when we returned to the palace. I gave Clarise and Samira a brief hug. Clarise responded politely, but Samira was puzzled and simply stood still. I assumed that she may be unaccustomed to the custom of hugging and simply said good night.

A week later, Majid made arrangements to take Randy to an international soccer meet being held at a stadium in the center of Riyadh. Majid had also invited his best friend, Ahmed. The three of them took a chauffeured stretch SUV to the stadium. Once the driver parked the vehicle, Majid escorted them into the building and up several flights of stairs lined with a red carpet. They entered a private enclosed suite, reserved for royalty. Majid stood in a line of young princes who were waiting to greet the most senior prince with a cordial kiss on the cheek. Once the ceremony had been observed, Majid showed his guests to their plush seats. A Filipino waiter brought them sodas and coffee. The guys stretched out and relaxed to watch the game.

Randy enjoyed watching Majid and Ahmed cheer enthusiastically for their team more than watching the game itself. Soccer, a national pastime, brought great pleasure and enjoyment into the young boys' lives. When the Saudi team won and the game was over, Majid rushed down to the field and greeted the members of the team whom he knew personally. Though Randy was nearly lost in the mob, he waited patiently for the young prince. At last, Majid returned and showed his guests back to the waiting van. Though the event was an enjoyable outing, Randy had noticed that only men had been allowed. There wasn't a single woman on the premises, but Majid quickly explained that we would get used to the situation.

As fall progressed, we decided to show the prince and princess how well Majid and Samira were doing. We planned a special open house to display their projects and papers. The children worked diligently to complete their assignments and prepare them for their parents. We gathered the projects and arranged them around the school. We mounted photos of the mock archeological dig done under Randy's supervision on the blue bulletin board. We hung the art projects Zoe had them do, a portrait of a Pharaoh and one of a jackal painted on papyrus, next to the photos. Clay models inscribed with their names in hieroglyphics were placed on the table next to their constructions of the pyramids. When we were done, we were all proud of our school.

Early the next evening, Randy and I joined Majid, Samira, Zoe, Luis, Abdullah, and Clarise and waited anxiously for Their Highnesses to arrive. When Majid heard the outer gate open, he rushed out to greet his parents. Abdullah was close on his heels.

"The second son," quipped someone behind me.

I turned around to see who had spoken so critically. The person shrugged his shoulders and said, "Even the prince's dog thinks he's a prince."

I winced at the criticism. I was learning that not everyone appreciated Abdullah.

The striking couple entered, the prince preceding the princess. The prince wore his long white *thobe* and *ghutra* and proudly emanated gentle, yet strong authority. Princess Noura shed her a*baya* to reveal a long, black wool skirt, smart black pumps and a red cashmere sweater. Diamond earrings with ruby centers dangled underneath her shoulder length dark hair. She wore a diamond-studded watch that was different from the one I had seen before.

Abdullah straightened his dark olive-green jacket and stood on his toes to greet the prince on the forehead with a traditional kiss. Unfortunately, he missed the prince's forehead and planted his lips on the prince's nose. The prince chuckled, and I was embarrassed for Abdullah. The royals proceeded around the room shaking hands and warmly greeting the staff members.

Majid and Samira had planned to take turns explaining their projects. Though academic success was something Samira had always been recognized for, it was new for Majid. When Majid started his presentation and his success was obvious, his excitement consumed him. His gifted skills as an orator took over and we witnessed how articulate the young prince could be. His father was so pleased with Majid's success that he called for other male relatives to join him and praise his son. Several dignified princes appeared and marveled over Majid's success. One of them especially admired the scaled model of the solar system and cycle of a star's life.

Samira looked dejected, but the powerful and intimidating princes outnumbered the teachers. We didn't know protocol for interrupting them on her behalf. Samira lingered in the background and gave way to Majid and the men as she had done so many times before.

After the presentation, the prince wanted to know what we would study next. When Randy said ancient China, ancient Greece and medieval Europe, the prince suggested we board a yacht and travel the world, leaning about each country.

Prince Faisal approached Abdullah for a brief conference, and Princess Noura met with the teachers. "I am so pleased. I knew my son could be reached," she said.

"But it didn't go exactly as planned, Your Highness," said Clarise.

"Samira didn't have a chance to explain her projects once Majid became so enthused," I said.

"I see. Majid," called the princess. He joined the small circle immediately. "My son, I am proud of your success, but your sister must have her chance to speak. This is her school too."

"But, Mama!"

The princess was firm yet kind. "Next time Samira will speak. Your father and I agree that in our family, everyone is treated equally."

Majid looked pleadingly into his mother's eyes and then relented. Samira smiled, and I was relieved that she was respected within her family. Finally, the prince and princess said good evening. The royals left the premises for their evening festivities at the palace.

The teachers gathered in the foyer and breathed a collective sigh of relief. I collapsed into the nearest chair. Zoe plopped down on the sofa next to me and looked pleased.

Clarise said, "The prince and princess loved it! They've never seen Majid so successful in school."

"I'm proud of their work," said Zoe, "and not just their art projects. Everything was great."

Abdullah joined us. I wanted his approval for the field trip to Egypt, but I was disheartened when he said that the prince wasn't fond of Egypt. Clarise offered to suggest it to the princess. Abdullah acknowledged Randy and told him to write a proposal so he could look it over.

Randy noticed the slight but retained his composure. "I've also got the original proposal you requested ready, plus a new one with suggestions about contacting universities. I want to get together with you and discuss the details."

Abdullah nodded. "Get back with me on it. Good job, everyone. Enjoy the rest of your evening." He excused himself and left.

Clarise explained that Saudis looked suspiciously upon Egypt since past political relations had been tenuous. When Gamel Nasser overthrew the Egyptian king and replaced the monarchy with a socialist state, he formed strong ties with the Soviet Union. * He also publicly criticized the Saudi royal family in the 1960s, claiming that Saudi oil fields belonged to all Arabs in the Middle East. When the Egyptian monarchy was toppled, King Faisal allowed Egyptian fundamentalists entry into Saudi Arabia, where they set up the fundamental *madrassas* schools and began preaching with anti-Western sentiment. Later, Saudi rulers feared the propaganda of the fundamentalists who had arisen during the 1980s and were responsible for the death of Anwar Sadat. However, since the trip was for the children's education on ancient Egyptian archaeology and artifacts, Clarise thought that the princess would approve.

Clarise suggested that we start planning a unit on China and another open house. Randy, Zoe and I agreed and decided to arrange it so Majid and Samira could each receive equal opportunity to shine. When we asked Clarise if the prince was serious about touring the world on a floating classroom, she shook her head, saying it was simply his way of expressing how impressed he was. We sighed with understanding and said good night.

Randy and I felt a great sense of professional satisfaction in our students' progress. Clarise supported our endeavors and applauded our success. Prince Faisal and Princess Noura were pleased. The proposal Randy finally submitted to Abdullah gave everyone a say, kept the peace and kept our school on the path to success. And I respected the integrity with which Randy handled a potentially awkward situation by including Clarise. With the teachers, administrators, and parents pulling together, we knew Majid and Samira would continue to flourish. We thanked God for giving us wisdom and causing us to prosper.

7.

BEDOUIN BEAUTY

PRINCESS SAMIRA WANTED me to see a beautiful side of Saudi Arabia. She was concerned that Americans stereotyped Arabs and cast everyone in the same light as Saddam Hussein. To enlighten me, she invited me to her cousin's wedding. Since I wanted to learn about every aspect of an Islamic woman's life, I eagerly accepted the invitation.

As the date approached, she sauntered upstairs humming. She entered the classroom with a dreamy look that glazed her eyes. "They are so much in love!"

"Who?" I asked, searching for her English file.

"My cousins who are getting married." She sank comfortably into the swivel chair humming the tune of a faintly familiar song.

"But aren't marriages arranged?" I asked, trying to recall the name of the tune.

"Most parents today won't make their kids marry someone they don't want to. At least, my dad would never do that."

I was happy to hear that most parents wouldn't force an unwanted marriage upon their children as had often been done in the days the *Bedouin* traversed the deserts with their tents and camel herds. But I also wondered how her cousins met if men and women were always separated. Samira said that because they were first cousins, they met at large family gatherings in the privacy of their homes. When they grew up, they fell in love. In fact, Samira's parents were first cousins as well.

"I will only marry a prince," she proclaimed, "because people outside our family don't understand our loyalty. And I'd never do what Princess Diana did and talk about family in public."

I said, "Western women work hard to have meaningful relationships with their husbands. I suspect she was searching for a kind of authenticity and loyalty herself. And you could end up marrying someone you take for granted."

But she thought her cousins were too immature. Indeed, Samira demonstrated maturity far beyond her young years. I told her how my husband and I were best friends, so we never thought about romance. All of a sudden we realized we were an ideal match, fell in love and became engaged on our third date.

She smiled. "You two make a sweet couple. There's something innocent about you. It makes me think Christians and Muslims can get along."

I was touched by her candid comment and marveled at her insight. Her acceptance and tolerance of a different religion surpassed the wisdom of the fundamental *imams* and clerics.

She continued, "The wedding will start at ten and last all night. I'll send my driver, Ali, to get you. Afterwards, you can stay over at my house. Do you have anything fancy to wear?"

Indeed, I had bought a gown in California. Daydreaming overtook me momentarily as I recalled the moment I found it. I had searched all over for something to wear on formal occasions overseas. I'd been in department stores and boutiques, up and down escalators and aisles looking for the right gown at the right price. I'd nearly given up when an elegant display caught my attention while walking out of Nordstroms. The sapphire sheen of one gown cast an alluring spell over me. Enchanted, I headed straight for it.

As I touched the lace shoulder, it seemed like a fairy tale from the past flew on its wings into my present and materialized before my eyes. The full organza skirt cascaded to the floor, shimmering like a midnight lake under a full summer moon. The lace bodice had cap sleeves and a scoop neckline. It hugged the waist where a large organza bow gathered the folds of the skirt.

Deciding to allow magic to interrupt my busy schedule, I found my size and waltzed into the dressing room. I slipped the dazzling blue beauty on and experienced a mid-life metamorphosis. I felt self-conscious about stepping out of the small dressing room to the three-way mirror, but indulgence was the key for the moment and I wanted every door to open. Though attending a royal wedding was a pipe dream, I wanted to be ready if invited. I tiptoed onto the platform. I turned this way and that, listening to the rustling layers of organza and taffeta, and decided to get it. My dream dress may have been 'off the rack,' but I felt as pretty as a princess in it.

Waking me from my daydream, Samira asked, "What color is it?"

"Blue, like a sapphire."

Her eyes lit up with girlish excitement. "My gown is powder blue with a scooped neckline and open V-back, and . . ."

I raised my eyebrows. "Your back shows?"

"Everyone dresses modern, and only women go to the wedding. The men have their own party at the groom's house or in the desert. The groom comes to the women's party for an hour. Then you should cover with a scarf. Anyway, my necklace is a large diamond choker with matching earrings and bracelet. It's the jewels that everyone talks about at the wedding. If you don't have any nice jewelry, Clarise has some sapphires and diamonds. Maybe she'll let you borrow them. I'll ask her. Clarise. Clarise!" Samira's voice reverberated throughout the hallways.

I cringed at the thought of asking Clarise for a personal favor.

Clarise walked calmly upstairs. "Can this wait until after class?"

"But, can Mrs. Decker borrow your sapphires for my cousin's wedding?"

I was embarrassed about the request, but if the jewels were important to Samira, I would wear them. Clarise politely agreed and told Samira to focus on her English lesson. The tardy bell rang before I could find her file. I felt so unorganized.

Several days later, Clarise brought her jewelry to school. Together, Clarise and Samira were softly singing. While I wanted to join them, I was too shy. Clarise carefully lifted the heirloom out of its box as Samira and I watched the gems shimmer in the overhead light. Small diamonds surrounded the oval sapphires. The choker length would be perfect for my neckline. Clarise put the jewels back into the case and handed them to me. I clasped the case tightly and thanked her. It was the first time I'd ever had the opportunity to wear such an expensive piece of jewelry. Clarise offered to contact a friend of hers, Francine, who would be attending the wedding also. Clarise thought it would be more enjoyable if I could visit with someone who spoke English while Samira paid her obligatory respects to her many relatives.

Later that afternoon I showed Randy the sapphires. He wanted to buy me something to go with them, especially since I had made so many sacrifices to live in the male-dominated culture. That evening we went to a nearby jewelry store. We couldn't afford the sapphire bracelet I'd seen while shopping with Lydia and Jan, so I picked out a ring with an oval sapphire and three small diamonds. It would be a lovely remembrance of the wedding.

When the day of the wedding arrived, I was too excited to nap, so I lounged around, did my nails and played around with my hair. Once I was dressed, Randy took pictures. Around 8:30 in the evening, Samira's driver, Ali, arrived to take me to the palace.

Randy kissed me good-bye, saying, "Have fun at the party. You're my princess."

Ali opened the door of a white Aurora. Feeling like I was living in a fairy tale, I carefully lifted the long folds of my gown and stepped into the back seat of the car where women always sat. I draped the black a*baya* around my shoulders.

Riding alone, I suddenly felt a wave of anxiety. I was about to spend an evening with the women of the Saudi royal family, some of the richest women in the world, who would be flaunting millions of dollars in diamonds and precious gems. I reminded myself that I was a beloved-child of God, a Western woman who may not have great wealth but who had opportunities to study and chose my own path in life. I was able to take care of myself without relying upon a male. These rights that I took for granted were rights most Saudi women could only dream about. These rights were my hidden jewels.

By the time Ali drove through the palace gates, I had composed myself. He opened the door and I stepped into the evening breeze. Fadwa, a palace servant, ushered me into Samira's private quarters. She asked me to wait in a large room. A big screen television was tuned to an American basketball game. I peeked into a dressing room stocked with beautiful gowns and dresses hanging on large racks. I wondered if these all belonged to Samira.

Fadwa returned and escorted me to a private salon. Samira and her cousin were having their hair styled by a young woman who looked like she may have been from Thailand. Samira was thrilled to see me and introduced her cousin, Hassa, who was visiting from Europe. Since both girls wanted to see my gown, I circled in place. The girls approved, and I was relieved. The young teens graciously included me in the conversation by asking about my teaching, my husband and my travels. They talked about the elite private school Hassa attended in Europe. Hassa was proud of her school, and I hoped Samira was proud of her American school and tutor.

When Samira finished styling her hair, we returned to the sitting room with the basketball game. Another servant entered with snacks and drinks on a silver tray. We nibbled on pita bread, hummus, a few date-filled pastries and sipped ice cold Pepsi.

Hassa was ready to put on her gown. A Parisian designer made it with silk fabric from Milan. Fadwa brought the stunning gown with double spaghetti straps that crossed in the back. The ivory background was embroidered with delicate blue flowers that had tiny yellow centers. The bodice clung to the waist and the skirt fell gently to the floor, blossoming slightly along the hemline. Hassa slipped it carefully

80

over her dark brown hair and smoothed it into place.

Next, Cora brought Samira's gown and slipped it gently over her head. Samira was no longer the typical teenage student dressed in trendy fashions arriving at the door of my classroom. She was now a beautiful and elegant young woman, a real princess. She turned around and studied herself critically in a three-way mirror. She smoothed her gown and twisted and turned until she was pleased with her profile.

Cora brought in a velvet box containing the jewels Samira would wear. The necklace was an intricately engraved gold band about an inch wide covered with an array of some thirty karats of diamonds. The bracelet was similar but thinner. Cora fastened the pieces on Samira. The diamonds caught the light and sparkled like stars as Samira admired them in the mirror.

I could only guess their value. I knew that millions of dollars were spent on the jewels worn by wealthy Saudi women. One of the ironies of Saudi Arabia is that while women have very few rights, they are entitled to their own money, bank accounts and jewels. The jewels were a sign of a woman's worth to her husband and guaranteed her survival should something happen to him.

With jewels adorned and gowns flowing, we left Samira's waiting room and stepped into the hallway. Cora brought a bottle of Chanel and a small brass burner spewing smoky incense. She held the incense burner close to Samira, so she could take a deep breath of the musty fragrance. Samira feathered her hair over the smoke. She turned around in a circle as Cora swept the smoky scent over her from head to toe. Next, Samira sprayed Chanel all over herself. The ritual done, we walked down a long corridor toward the main entry.

Outside, we wrapped our *abayas* over our gowns. A silver Rolls Royce and blue BMW were parked in front of the palace. The back seat of the Rolls was enclosed with a black curtain. Samira's mother, Princess Noura, stepped out of the Rolls with her beautiful younger sister, Princess Sara. I noticed that Princess Noura had not yet dressed for the wedding. Samira kissed her mother good-bye as Sara, Samira and Hassa got into the back seat of the Rolls. The driver closed the curtains and shut the door securely. Cora, Fadwa and I crowded into the back of a BMW.

Cora smiled and asked, "Have you ever been to a wedding like this before?"

"No, I can't even imagine what it will be like."

"Then I will explain everything to you. I've been to many of these. I'm a little tired of going now because we are up all night."

"Do you know Clarise's friend, Francine?" I asked.

"I have met her at the school and will help you look for her. She has worked here for many years and is a very nice lady."

Cora was one of the more thoughtful and considerate servants working at the palace, and I was grateful that I would be able to visit with her even if I never found Clarise's friend.

Our cavalcade left the palace and drove along the well-lit city streets to the Intercontinental Hotel. Long lines of Mercedes Benzes, Jaguars, Rolls Royces and BMWs pulled up to the hotel entrance. Our chauffeurs opened the car doors for us and left us in front of the lobby. We followed several dozen covered women through heavily guarded doorways and entered the hidden world of Arabian women.

Once inside, we removed our dreary coverings. We were surrounded by dozens of lovely women in gowns of satin, chiffon, silk and beaded rayon in shades and hues from every facet of a rainbow. The women were draped in the most stunning diamonds I had ever seen. We walked down gold-carpeted corridors that were lined with hundreds of servants. Most of them were women from countries like Ethiopia, Sudan, Thailand, India and Pakistan, in service to royal family members and wives of wealthy businessmen.

Princess Sara led our entourage toward the ballroom. At the entry, she paused and made sure we were all with her. She nodded toward me, signaling me to enter with her and the two young princesses. Though I only saw her at the wedding, I will always remember how she made me feel welcome in an unfamiliar setting. Suddenly Samira, Hassa, and Sara disappeared into the immense crowd of royal women. Fadwa waved at a friend across the room and walked toward her. I followed Cora through the crowded ballroom, trying to absorb every fabulous detail.

The accommodations weren't what I expected. I thought we would enter a religious sanctuary, but the wedding was held in a hotel ballroom. The walls were draped in ivory chiffon. Sparkling crystal chandeliers hung from the ceiling. Instead of an altar, one end of the room had an elevated platform covered with a myriad of white roses, daisies and mums. In front of the flowers, a female band sang romantic Saudi melodies. The scent of incense and Chanel permeated the air all around me.

Rows of white chairs faced the aisle of the bridal procession rather than the front platform. The seats along the aisle were reserved for royal family members. Behind these seats were several rows for friends of the family and those Western professionals the royals employed. Nannies and servants, holding everything their princesses might need during a wedding, were relegated to seats against the wall. The arrangement inside reflected the classed society outside of the hotel walls.

Cora found seats in the middle where we would both feel comfortable. Some servants were dressed in yellow satin dresses with white trim. Others were dressed in their finest long dresses and bedecked with gold necklaces and bracelets. Cora explained that gold was frequently given as gifts to everyone from the bride's father at the time of a wedding. The women made their rounds offering us a variety of candies and cookies from tiered silver platters. Later we were served strong teas and Arabian coffee flavored with cardamom.

The royals were laden with dazzling jewels, both young and old, grandmother and teenager alike. Many women wore chokers of sparkling white diamonds with multiple strands dangling from the choker in a wide variety of graceful patterns. Others wore diamonds with emeralds, rubies or sapphires. Earrings were worn long, often with three descending gems dangling from the ear, completely surrounded by white diamonds.

Cora pointed to an older princess with graying black hair who was just entering the ballroom. She wore a low-cut black velvet gown. The emeralds and diamonds around her slender neck were far grander than anyone's in the room. Many princesses lined up to greet her. I wondered who she was and why these women seemed so fond of her. I admired their sincere warmth for one another.

I was glad to have a chance to visit with Cora and get to know her better. She had always been warm and welcoming, so I asked if she had family in Saudi.

"No," she said, "my daughter and son live in Malaysia with my husband, but I go home every summer. I'm working in Saudi to send my daughter to college. This spring she will finish her studies at law school."

Cora's eyes beamed with pride over her daughter's accomplishments. I was amazed at how many times I had met men and women who left family members in their homeland for work in Saudi Arabia.

"Has raising Samira eased the pain of living away from your own children?" I asked.

"In some ways, yes, because I've cared for her since she was an infant. Now Samira knows who she is and who I am. But her mother is good to me. When my father was ill, she let me return to care for him. Now, over there is Samira's favorite aunt, Princess Noura. And there's Samira's mother in the red satin gown."

I followed Cora's gaze and saw Princess Noura walking genteelly down the aisle in a strapless gown. Her diamond and ruby necklace sparkled as she stretched out her hand and warmly greeted women along the aisle. Her brown hair was scooped up into a chignon at the top of her head and pinned in place with a diamond-studded clasp.

Around eleven o'clock, the bride began her long walk down the aisle to the tune of a Saudi love song. The bride's pearl white gown was covered with lace from her shoulders to her feet. The full skirt fell gracefully from her tiny waist. The long, sheer veil was trimmed with lace and embroidered flowers along the edges, but I could still see the V-shaped back of the dress that ended at the waist with a large satin bow. Her brilliant diamond necklace and earrings formed a near halo around her happy face. She beamed like a bride deeply in love.

The princesses nodded their approval as the bride passed by. Several three and four year old girls followed behind her spreading flower petals along the carpet. She made her way to the platform and sat in a white satin chair. Her many relatives lined up to wish her happiness. The guests danced and sang in celebration around her. Samira was also dancing near the bride. Soon, Samira, Hassa and an unfamiliar young girl approached Cora and me.

"Did you see the bride, Mrs. Decker?" asked Samira.

"Oh, yes. She's as beautiful as you said she'd be."

Samira smiled and introduced her cousin, Maha.

"It's nice to meet you, Maha," I said extending my hand. The young princess shook my hand.

Samira encouraged me to join the dancing in the aisles. Behind me, women held their hands gracefully in the air swaying to the music of the band. Though nervous, I promised to try. The three young girls wandered off arm-in-arm toward a group of young women at the other end of the hall.

An hour later, the groom walked down the aisle with his father and four groomsmen. They were clad in white *thobes*. Their *ghutras* were white and held in place by intertwining black and gold bands. The six men remained aloof. As they marched down the aisle, women took out their scarves and covered their heads and gowns. However, the groom didn't notice them; his eyes were riveted on his beautiful bride at the end of the room. He too had the look of genuine love written upon his face. Happiness for this couple rose in my heart, and I whispered a prayer for a blessed future together.

The bride and groom sat side by side for a brief ceremony performed by an elderly religious man. The music, dancing and laughter drowned out the ceremony, but many of us watched the ceremony intently from a distance. The groom and his entourage left within the hour, and the celebration continued without them.

I put off using the restroom because it would be crowded and flooded with water. Instead of using toilet paper, women used water from spray hoses for cleansing, and the excess water flooded the entire floor. Around two in the morning, I couldn't wait any longer. Cora and I headed for the rest room where we encountered a long, long line. Cora and I waited for nearly half an hour and then battled streams of water on the floor. Unfortunately, the hem of my gown and my shoes became soaked, but at least I had brought a pack of tissues. The royals had booked private rooms in the hotel and now I wished I had done the same.

As we were returning to the hall, someone called out my name. "Kristin!"

Startled to hear my name in such a crowded place, I turned abruptly around and stared into the face of a strange Western woman with gorgeous red hair piled on top of her head. A few twirled strands surrounded her face and chin. Her emerald green satin gown swirled around her feet. A tall brunette in a stunning gold gown stood next to her clasping a gold-sequined bag and smiling.

"I'm Francine," said the stranger with red hair. Her accent was French. "Clarise asked me to look out for you since this is the first time you've been to a wedding. How are you managing?"

"Just fine. Cora and I are thoroughly enjoying our time. She's explaining everything to me."

Francine had met Cora previously at the school, so they embraced. Francine introduced her friend, Terry, who was from Australia and was working for the queen. The four of us decided to sit together for the remainder of the wedding. We discussed our travels, our new jobs and the unique opportunity to learn firsthand about Saudi Arabia. We agreed it was far better than merely reading about the country. Terry and I were also amazed to learn we had attended the same university in Canada. We reminisced about our university days and the times we had skipped lectures and snuck off to the grandeur of the Rockies to ski, figure skate and hike the backcountry. To find ourselves on the other side of the world, traversing dry desert sands and working for the Saudi royal family, was an unexpected turn of events for both of us.

Dinner was served at three a.m. We followed a crowd of several hundred women to the banquet halls. The hall was filled with numerous dining tables, buffet tables and an amazing spread of food from around the world. We found a remote buffet table, filled our plates with shrimp shish kebabs, lamb, salmon, chicken and a variety of salads. We sat at a large, round table and continued our conversation.

After the main course, I walked to the dessert tables. I passed an old, wrinkled servant digging into one of the fruit pies with her fingers. Appalled, I skipped dessert, returned to our table, and told my new friends that I'd seen a servant eating right out of the dish. Francine explained that some servants came from remotely rural villages in Saudi, Africa and Indonesia and had never been instructed in etiquette or hygiene.

We returned to the wedding hall and continued talking and laughing into the early morning hours. I was now quite comfortable and having a great time. Around 5 o'clock, Samira found Cora and I and said she was ready to leave. Sadly, I said good night to my new friend and followed Samira toward the hotel entrance. We pulled the long, drab robes over our glimmering evening gowns and entered the world that men ruled.

Finally, Ali drove through the palace gates. We dragged ourselves out of the car. Samira led me to a private villa that was next to the one Clarise used. When she asked if I had a good time, I kissed her on the forehead and said, "I will never forget it."

"I'm glad. Sleep in because we won't get up until noon."

I thanked her as she walked back down the stairs. I entered the private villa and saw that the bed sheets were already turned down and that a glass of water and some date cookies were set out on a bedside table. In the large adjoining marble bathroom, I draped my gown over a hanger. I took one last gaze at it. I had yet to sleep on this night of nights. It was now well past five o'clock, and I noticed the sky turning light. I crawled wearily into bed. For once the loudspeakers did not awaken me. Early morning prayer had long since been over. I fell asleep thanking God for making it possible for me to attend such a wonderful and memorable event. It gave me an intimate look into the life of my student and left me admiring Saudi women and how they coped with their lives without men.

8.

FORBIDDEN!

FOLLOWING THE WEDDING I was delighted to spend occasional free time with Samira and Maha. They were like teenage girls anywhere. Their musical tastes were both Western and Middle Eastern, and I grew to love the haunting melodies of their Middle Eastern love songs. Inevitably, their gossip centered on other girls and how to meet boys. Single men and women were never allowed to commingle, and I was about to learn the desperate measures youngsters could take to find true love. I also saw how religious fundamentalism could damage lives, hinder authentic relationships and deny basic human need.

Maha had invited Clarise, Samira and I for lunch and a shopping spree, so within several days, Randy dropped me off at Maha's palace. I was disappointed to learn that Samira cancelled at the last minute. Since Clarise had been warming up to Randy and me, I put my suspicions about her aside for the time being.

Maha was dressed in blue jeans and a white lace blouse and looked like an angel. I noticed an unusual prance in her steps. After polite greetings, we headed toward her car. She chattered excitedly as we climbed in. Maha said something in Arabic to her driver and we sped off through the palace gates.

"We'll have lunch first," she said, "A guy will be there, but his dad runs the restaurant."

Her comment about a male attending was confusing. I couldn't understand why Maha would include a male relative on the shopping trip. Clarise cast me an alarmed look, and Maha rummaged through her purse for her cell phone. When she made a call, Clarise leaned forward and whispered, "This is no shopping trip. She's meeting a guy!"

Dear Lord, help us! I cried in my heart. Maha had arranged a date, and Clarise and I had been tricked into going along. No wonder Samira had cancelled, and Clarise looked so distressed. I could feel my heart thumping wildly.

When Maha hung up the phone, she was beaming. "I'm crazy about this boy. He's so cute."

Clarise stiffened. "Maha, you can not meet a boy. It's strictly forbidden!"

Maha was unfazed. "Don't worry. The restaurant is closed, and the boy has guards watching for *mutawwa*. With you two around, it will look perfectly innocent. I wouldn't invite you if I thought something awful would happen."

Clarise and I had no authority over a determined princess. I had no idea what to do but begged God to help us get out of the situation. If Clarise and I went along with Maha's plan and were caught, we could be abruptly deported. Maha's fate could be much worse because the family would consider a clandestine meeting between an unmarried male and female a horrendous act of dishonor. Maha could face either death by stoning or lifelong isolation in the infamous 'woman's room,' where she would be confined without human contact. Frantically, I tried to think of a way out of our predicament and resigned myself to the fact that Clarise and I would have to work together for everyone's benefit.

Maha sensed my anxiety and spoke calmly. "We will be perfectly safe."

"This is not a good idea," I warned. "Your mother would be devastated. You know that women who've been caught have been married off to old men or drowned in a pool. Do you want to be a fourth wife?"

"Don't you think Saudi kids do this all the time? Besides, this date will be chaperoned."

"Mrs. Decker and I could be blamed!" exclaimed Clarise indignantly.

I was curious to know how she met the boy. She said it was the way they all met boys. They were brothers of girlfriends, and friends of theirs were always sneaking them boy's phone numbers. When driving along the streets or passing one another in the malls, an older brother usually grabbed the number.

Looking at Clarise, I pleaded with my eyes, *Do something*! She looked empathically toward me and nodded.

Maha's driver pulled into the restaurant parking lot and drove to the back entrance. Two watchful Saudi men stood by the kitchen entrance with mobile phones in hand. They motioned to our driver to move closer to the door.

Maha ordered us to cover our heads and faces as she waited for the guards to give the signal. In an instant, they ushered us out of the car and whisked us through the kitchen door. We were escorted to a corner dining table hidden discreetly behind a screen. At the head was a handsome young teen in a white *thobe* and *ghutra*. He greeted us with a proud smile and gazed lovingly at Maha without ever touching her. The waiters seated us and handed each of us a menu.

Clarise set her menu on the table and clutched her stomach. "Oh, I'm feeling sick."

Noticing her discomfort, the young gentleman said, "I hope you're alright." His English was polished, and his manners impeccable.

Clarise's face turned extremely pale. Suddenly, she bolted her head over her knees, gagged and then vomited all over the tile floor.

"Oh, my God!" screamed Maha. Her boyfriend blurted something loudly in Arabic. Everyone but Clarise charged out of the chairs and stood back as far as possible. The smell was horrendous and the boy was frantically cleaning remnants that had flown onto his pressed white *thobe*. He snapped his fingers at a nearby waiter who set down his tray and gathered the linens to clean up.

At last Clarise sat up and addressed the boy. "I'm so sorry, but we'll have to go."

"Indeed, I believe you must." He tried to mask his disgust with compassion and motioned for the guards. We were whisked through the kitchen to our car. The driver spun quickly around on the gravel. Maha cast a weary, disappointed smile to the boy who stood discreetly at the kitchen door. He waved and smiled through his disappointment.

Once alone in the car, I wondered if Maha would be angry at Clarise for ruining her date. I was surprised to see her turn to Clarise with deep concern and affection. She said it must have been God's will. She slumped into her seat and remained quiet for the rest of the ride, but I began to breathe more easily.

The driver dropped Maha off at her palace and then took Clarise and me to my compound where I could tend to her. Randy wasn't home, so I settled Clarise down on our sofa.

When I asked Clarise if she was all right, a mischievous smile crossed her face. "More or less. When I leaned over, I stuck my finger down my throat as far as I could to make myself throw up. Now I do feel awful."

I had wondered how we'd manage a princess for her own good and felt a new respect for Clarise. God had worked providentially, so no one lost face or was harmed.

"Don't ever tell her, Samira or their mothers. If any of the family patriarchs learn of this episode, they'll be furious. It would be a complete loss of face."

"Maha's mother would appreciate your intervention, and someday Maha will, too."

"I hope so, but I'm worried about her. She's desperate for a boyfriend because she doesn't want to end up like an older cousin."

Thinking of the rich life of luxury a princess must lead, I wondered why. Clarise explained that Maha's cousin was married and had children, but her husband was usually out of the country on business and had another wife. Some Saudi men saw marriage just for sex and children, like in the old harem days when numerous wives and concubines were kept for the pleasure of the patriarch. Though Mohammed had approved additional wives, his approval was in the context of war widows whose husbands had died in battle. The practice had deviated from its root purposes, and deep relationships with the opposite sex were something many people didn't experience or expect. Maha's cousin felt isolated, and there were so many like her that they took each other on as lovers. Her cousin was one of the most notorious lesbian princesses in Riyadh.

"But I thought lesbian relationships were against the religion," I said.

"All homosexual acts are, but since they are punishable by death, these liaisons are a well-kept secret. I suppose when human need for care and affection is dismissed, rules are worthless."

"But," I protested, "when we're driving, I look over at other cars. I see husbands smiling and talking affectionately with their wives, and I sense love between them."

"That's the more modern Saudi family. Multiple wives aren't really the norm anymore because each one is to be treated equally and that's rarely practical. But arranged marriages don't mean love can't develop."

"But marriages according to the old school . . ."

". . . can be like a prison sentence," finished Clarise. "I've heard so many tragic stories, even stories of women, especially women from the Philippines, Pakistan and India, being held as sex slaves."

Before leaving California, I talked with a colleague who came from the Philippines. Her father had been assigned as ambassador to Saudi Arabia for the expressed purpose of protecting Filipina women who had gone to Saudi as servants and ended up enslaved and raped. Often they were held in grimy, unhealthy conditions without a refuge. I wondered how many other women were held captive by those designated to protect them or were drowning in their splendor, wealth and isolation.

Women lived lives completely segregated from the world of men. Businesses and homes alike had separate accommodations for them. In their homes, women had designated quarters where their lives revolved around each other, their children and their assigned night with the husband. Rumors abounded that secret harems harbored women from third world countries and kept them as sex slaves. Perhaps the colleague I worked with in Los Angeles had been telling me the truth after all.

Maha's innocent rendezvous made complete sense to me now, and my heart went out to her. My thoughts turned to Maha and Samira's futures. What kind of men would they marry? Could they find happiness in such a rigid and structured system like the lucky bride whose wedding we had all recently attended?

Clarise said, "At least I have some good news. I met someone! Last summer, I noticed a good-looking guy at the airport. Then I ran into him registering at the embassy. It seemed meant when a mutual friend introduced us at an embassy event. He's from America and is a pilot for a private airline that flies dignitaries around the world. If only Samira and Maha knew!"

I was thrilled she had made such a great connection. She and her boyfriend planned to attend a Halloween party being held for Westerners the next evening. The party was technically illegal because men and women would commingle. Since it would be held in a secure location, we weren't overly concerned and looked forward to a relaxing time with friends.

Neither Clarise nor I had had time to find a Halloween costume. We realized that our time was now free, so we decided to go shopping after all. I called Jan and learned that she still needed a costume and was eager to join us. Our afternoon had been redeemed, and I found myself hoping Clarise and I could put our disagreements behind us and form a friendship.

After a short rest, Clarise called Akbar to pick us up. Driving in Saudi was unnerving enough, but with someone like Akbar at the wheel it could be a thrill ride. His speedometer was set to ring a warning at speeds over sixty-five, but he habitually ignored it, cruising the wide boulevards at speeds over eighty. He swung in and out of traffic, dodging drivers as aggressive as he, in what seemed the male population's quest to prove their manhood. Akbar's chest swelled with pride as he cut off drivers, ignored traffic lanes, made left-hand turns from the far right lane and squeezed between cars with barely an inch to spare. After a nasty near miss, Jan yelled at Akbar to slow down.

"Sorry, Miss." At last, other cars sped by and the obnoxious ringing of the speedometer stopped. I was glad Jan had the courage to say something. For a few moments Akbar's driving inched closer to sanity. Suddenly, his speed and swerving increased again.

Jan pleaded with him. "Akbar! We're scared. And it's making me sick."

"But, Miss, those boys bad." Akbar nodded toward a car on our right. Looking out the side window, we saw a small white Toyota speed up and slow down, attempting to match Akbar's speed. Four teenage boys were in the car, and now that we noticed them, they began blowing kisses our way and driving even more erratically. Akbar reached into the console for a knife.

"For goodness sakes, Akbar. Put that away," ordered Clarise.

"They dangerous, ma'am. I know this kind." Though I was relieved Akbar was willing to protect us, he also made me worry about the boys' motives. They continued their antics with increasing lewdness. Remembering how Majid and his friend took a baseball bat to protect Samira on our drive to the restaurant, I shuddered.

Jan gave the youngsters a dirty look. "They're so annoying! What do you bet they watch Western TV and think all women act like the ones on *Baywatch*?"

We turned away from the window in disgust and pulled our scarves tighter around our faces. Akbar kept one eye on their car, one on the road ahead and his hand on his knife. Clarise suggested that we ignore them, as she'd seen kids behave like this before. She figured they'd reach their turnoff and forget about us. Sure enough, the boys soon grew tired of their sport and turned off of the highway several minutes later. Relieved, we continued our journey in silence.

Akbar let us off on a street corner and waited by the car. Even though he was allowed to drive us around, he wasn't allowed to accompany us shopping. I always felt safe around him, and fortunately he kept his eyes on us for as long as possible. At least Clarise, Jan and I could stick together. Clarise led the way toward the hundreds of racks that lined the sidewalks ahead.

The outdoor shopping center was somewhat like a flea market. The Junk *Souk,* as it was known, operated like a thrift store full of old party dresses formerly belonging to princesses and wealthy women. After searching for nearly an hour, and laughing over some of the more outlandish creations, we each found a suitable costume. Clarise decided to dress as a nightclub singer and Jan as a clown. I found a dress with lots of gold beadwork gracing the neckline in an ancient Egyptian fashion. Perhaps I could cover my hair and go as Cleopatra. Since dressing rooms were illegal in all shops, boutiques and malls, we couldn't try them on. We would have to wait until we got home. If they didn't fit though, we wouldn't be out much money. When we returned to our car, I was glad to see Akbar waiting faithfully.

By the time we returned to the compound, it was late afternoon. Extra security guards had been posted along the entrance and main streets. Dozens of very expensive foreign cars were parked outside the restaurant near the conference center. They were out of place in the predominately middle-class environment.

Akbar dropped Jan off at her villa, but Clarise wanted a cup of tea to settle her stomach, so he let us off at the restaurant. We left Akbar to tend to the car. He took out a cloth and began cleaning the dust off of the windows.

The host seated us near large windows with a view of the pool. We were surprised to see several Saudi men lounging around the patio tables talking, smoking and laughing. In their *thobes* and *ghutras*, they looked out of place on the compound, but sauntered around like they owned it. A waiter came and took our order. We asked for hot tea and date cookies, and then curiosity got the best of me. I asked him why the Saudis were on our compound. He looked down at the floor and said that the men were friends of the owner.

Suddenly Clarise pointed out the window. "Look! A blonde on the arm of a Saudi. You can't miss her. She's in that red sequined gown by the pool."

I scanned the patio looking for her. When our eyes met, I couldn't read them. She was emotionally distant, as if numb to her own feelings. "I thought everyone knew how Saudi men treat women," I said. "Did you hear about the journalist whose husband beat her so badly she ended up in the hospital?"

"Yes, I read about it in a magazine. These women on the patio must be in it for the money," sighed Clarise. "The Saudis pay outrageous sums of money for their entertainment."

The waiter returned with our cups of tea and shortbread cookies filled with dates.

"Did you hear about the Saudi yacht party off the coast of New York City?" Clarise asked.

I poured my cup of tea. "Was it in the news?"

"Oh, no. I learned about it from someone who was actually on the yacht. Apparently some Saudi businessmen had New York prostitutes brought on board for an all night fling, but when the party was over, they threw the women overboard and let them drown at sea. The eyewitness became so sick, he vomited all over his room and vowed never to go anywhere with Saudis again. It was his gut reaction to the events that gave his account credibility."

Though I'd heard similar rumors, I had always hoped they weren't true. The growing number of stories was disheartening. I had hoped to hear evidence to the contrary rather than a confirmation.

In spite of how the day started, Clarise and I had made the best of it. We had gotten to know one another better and started a friendship. I began to regret my elation when Abdullah had asked us to keep an eye on her expenditures. Feeling patronized by Clarise wasn't enough of a reason to become Abdullah's pawn in a game of palace intrigue.

Princess Noura expected Clarise at the palace soon, so we gathered our packages and left. Outside, I saw a security guard I knew standing at the door of the conference room where the Saudis were gathering. When I greeted him, he looked away. Two young women walked passed him and entered the room. Music blasted through the door, as did a pungent mixture of incense and alcohol.

"Ma'am, you go now," snapped Seid.

"Why? Saudis shouldn't even be here," I said.

His face turned dark red. "Ma'am, I am sorry. These ladies are prostitutes. They flash me. Under the black cover they wear nothing. Please, go."

I knew Seid had a wife, three children and ailing parents in India who depended on his paycheck. Clarise and I left shaking our heads, especially because the women seemed so young. We reached the curbside where Akbar was patiently waiting. We said good-bye and agreed to meet up at the Halloween dance.

The next evening, I dressed for the illegal party. Randy and I picked up Mike and Jan and drove off the compound to a private estate. When we entered the mansion, we were led down a secret stairwell where our IDs were checked by American and British security guards.

Finally we emerged into an underground disco. The far wall was a window that provided an underground view of a swimming pool. The pool's soft lighting created a romantic ambience. A Western band was setting up on a corner stage. A polished wood dance floor with a glitter ball was in the center. A magnificent buffet lined the wall. Waiters rushed about making sure everything was just right. Along the dance floor were dining tables and chairs where couples were being seated. Jan and Mike were gathered around one of the larger tables with Zoe and her husband, Brian. Bottles of freshly brewed "tea" were in the center of the table. Clarise and her fiancé, Hunter, soon joined us, and Clarise proudly introduced him.

Befriending us, Hunter said, "Nearby there's a British pub with a picture of the Queen on the wall. It's a well-guarded secret, but if you want to go, I can arrange it."

"Sure," said Randy. Mike and Brian asked to be counted in.

Jan said, "I heard there are secret church services, and prayer meetings too."

"We went to a secret service. Bibles are contraband, but they had them," said Hunter.

Randy shook his head. "Geez, church is illegal, Bibles are illegal, alcohol is illegal, mixed company is illegal."

"Dating is illegal," added in Clarise. We laughed with her and Hunter.

"But every religion has its own list of forbidden behaviors," Zoe said.

"Speaking of forbidden behavior, did you guys hear about the Saudi sex party on our compound?" asked Mike. "The resident's committee plans to discuss it with the management. We have to think of the children who live there."

I said, "Some of the prostitutes looked like children. I walked right passed them."

Brian added, "Some of the workers spied on them through the roof. They could see everything through the glass dome. Each Saudi had four or five women to himself, and they made lap-dancing look innocent."

"Don't they know we can figure out what's going on?" Jan asked.

"Maybe they think that's how everyone parties," Zoe said.

"Well, when severe restrictions don't allow for natural human need to be met, it's going to find a way out somehow," said Randy.

"That's a little too Freudian for me," said Mike, laughing somewhat uncomfortably.

"I wonder how they justify that attitude toward women?" asked Zoe.

Clarise said, "They use the *Qur'an* to teach that women are inferior and weak."

Jan said, "Great, so men just make it worse for women. One of our students told me, 'Men have special needs.' That made me wonder what kind of relationships they have with women. I get the idea that married Muslim women are on an untouchable pedestal, but all other women are looked at like prostitutes."

"Making spiritual love good but physical love evil," I added. "That splits our personalities. But every culture seems to struggle with how to integrate sexuality into our lives. We forget God came up with the whole idea."

Randy agreed. "All these religious rules remind me somewhat of growing up Baptist. We couldn't go to movies, smoke or drink, and I wasn't allowed to dance." Randy related how the rules just created a front that made them arrogant and uncaring, phony and judgmental. As a child, he was taught that the Lutherans and Catholics were all going to hell. In his church, the need to be doctrinally right was more important than loving God or neighbor. Randy became so caught up in 'getting his life right with God,' that it took him years to realize he'd never be good enough to earn His favor anyway.

"What's interesting to me," said Clarise, "is that Islam doesn't believe in original sin.

"Whoa," said Mike. "Original sin?"

"The belief that human kind is alienated from God and unable to do good without his intervention," explained Randy.

"Without a redeeming faith that changes our human nature," I added.

"Right," continued Clarise. "Islamic scholars believe humans are born in a state of innocence and purity."

"So there's no need for any kind of redemption from sin?" asked Mike.

"Or a Savior or Messiah," said Randy.

"As a result, Muslims focus on correct behavior rather than correct belief or doctrine. The *Qur'an* clearly states that ones good deeds must outweigh the bad deeds. It's in chapter, or *Surah*, 23

"Well, how do they know they're going to make it to Heaven?" asked Jan.

"They don't," said Randy. "Unless they die a death of a martyr."

"So instead of God sending his son to die for us, Allah expects people to die for him?" asked Zoe.

"Yes," said Clarise.

"That's the result of believing you can earn you way into Heaven," I said.

"I looked that up in a copy that Samira gave me. I found it in chapter, or *Surah* 23:102," I added.

"But the gap between rules and the perversion is so blatantly obvious," said Mike. "Whatever these religious groups are doing isn't showing the results they say they value."

"That's true of every religion when it's legalistic rather than heartfelt," said Randy. "When I went to seminary, I finally learned the only thing that could change me was grace at the cross of Christ. Every day I remind myself that I stand before God on grace alone. There I finally found peace."

Through my studies, I had learned that legalism in any religion, whether Christian, Jewish, Hindi or Islamic, created two classes of people, those who kept the rules and those who didn't. The group that kept the rules began to feel more righteous and superior to the others. Legalism thereby became the author of self-righteousness and sabotaged mercy. The only antidote to spiritual pride that I knew of was God's mercy and grace. Grace, the everlasting kindness and love of God, is extended to everyone and places the entire human race on an equal plane. Grace is for those considered degenerate, perverse and hypocritical. The innocent and perfect feel no need for grace. Judaic scholars who understand God's teachings on Messiah also understand the *chesed* grace and loving-kindness.

I had decided that people of faith didn't need to agree with one another to care for one another. Christians, Muslims and Jews could be modeling acceptance and forgiveness to the world instead of fighting with each other to be doctrinally right or to control various holy sites. We are all made in His image, and we each have a heritage in God and a place for mercy in our teachings, our scriptures and our lives. We have the power, and indeed the example in scriptures, to move beyond tolerance to a greater love for each other. Grace gives us the power to love those who are different and even those we consider outcasts and enemies.

Whenever I thought of the parable of the prodigal son in the New Testament book of Luke, I had a deepened sense of God's grace. A man had two grown sons who requested their share of his inheritance while he was still living. One restless son left the family with his share of the inheritance in hand. He searched for fulfillment in lascivious ways and ended up squandering his father's wealth on drink and women. When he had reached a point of despair and found himself groveling in a pig sty, he realized he would be better off working as a servant for his father. With that he returned. When the father saw his son returning, he rejoiced and welcomed the son with open arms. Over the objections of the older son who had always kept his father's rules, the father celebrated the homecoming of the wayward son. Likewise, whatever I did, I knew God was standing with open arms waiting to receive me into His presence. He took away my guilt and shame, clothed me in righteousness and made a place for me in his kingdom. In fact, it was the concept of grace that distinguished the Christian faith from others and compelled me to become a Christian. Grace had ended my search among the philosophies and religions of the world for peace with God.

Apart from grace, I also realized that the only alternative to legalism was to believe that there was no moral code to adhere to whatsoever. Though the dissolution of absolutes wove a pattern throughout the history of philosophy and influenced many cultures, I had found the absence of a moral code to be as destructive and meaningless as religious legalism; as well as ineffective in assuaging guilt. Though it was disguised as freedom in the arts and politics of the Western world, the absence of morality was actually bondage that carried with it the potential to damage lives and deny one's freedom to choose good.

As I studied theology and its intertwining relationship with philosophy, I came to agree with the great Reformation theologian, Martin Luther, and his 4th century mentor, St. Augustine. Both of the scholars based their writings on Paul the Apostle. Our human wills were held captive to a fallen nature and apart from the crucifixion, inextricably bound to sin and evil. Grace was the only empowering liberation to perversion and destruction. Its regenerating power enabled me, through the Holy Spirit, to make authentic and ethical decisions. Furthermore, it was the only antidote to my own hypocrisy, arrogance and boasting before a Holy God. Grace was the deep abiding sense of utter and complete forgiveness that provided the experience of freedom, cleanliness and boldness before the holy, everlasting and accessible God of the universe. It left me in awe of the God of Abraham, Isaac and Jacob and wiped out my arrogant boasting of righteousness. Grace made me grateful for my redemption through his son, the Messiah, Christ Jesus.

Waking me from my reverie, Randy leaned over and asked, "How about the first dance, sweetheart?"

I extended my hand graciously toward my adoring husband. He grasped it and whisked me onto the dance floor. We freely swayed to the rhythms of the live band and temporarily dismissed the fact that we could be arrested for being among mixed company. After witnessing the extent to which legalism could damage lives, I felt especially grateful for the husband God had given me. I respected his insight and decency. Raising my hands into the air, I watched my new gold bangles that he'd given me glisten under the lights.

I pulled him closer but still hoped I could find the courage to overcome old embedded anxieties that seemed to be surfacing lately. I wanted to reach out to him emotionally, and trust him with my heart. In spite of grace, it still seemed like an unknown psychological barrier held a part of me captive, making it difficult to be vulnerable and tell my husband how much I really needed him. In fact, I didn't even believe he really loved me as he said. I couldn't experience his love completely, hold onto it and enjoy it. I wondered where the emotional wall originated from and how I would overcome it. A complete liberation in my human relationships seemed to be an ongoing and complicated process.

9.

INTO THE VALLEYS

ON THE WEEKENDS, Randy and I liked to spend time with other Americans and explore points of interest. We invited Mike and Jan to join us on an afternoon trip because they were worried about their next teaching assignment. They weren't sure Abdullah would acquire the necessary exit visas in time so they'd be able to attend international job fairs. We wanted to be the kind of friends around whom they could safely blow off a little steam, but we also hoped to encourage them to resolve their concerns diplomatically, so they could relax and enjoy the rest of their time in Saudi.

Riyadh was built on an escarpment, and neighbors assured us that an excursion to the rims of the nearby desert wonder was worth it. As we drove beyond the city limits, I worried about clearing the civil police road check. We had our papers and permits, but I feared the police might harass us because of our dogs and the mixed company in the car. But the check was routine and the policeman's demeanor was welcoming. I assumed that he wasn't worried about four fair-skinned, blonde-haired Westerners who looked like family. As we continued along the modern highway, several Saudi families with small children smiled and waved at the dogs.

Before long, the road began to wind down through tall cliffs. Ancient rivers had created deep gorges through the high and ruddy plateaus. The gorges later became camel trade routes, and the modern highway cut through the rock along the same path. * Looking back, we saw towering ridges and rocky pinnacles protruding the skyline. Amongst them, deep gorges opened like fans onto the sandy plains below. We traveled along the valley floor admiring the miles of jutting escarpment formations. Jade green grass and straw-like weeds sprouted from wisps of adobe colored sand. Camel and goat herds grazed in the distance under lone acacia trees.

Finally we pulled over and parked off the road. Aslan and Cheyenne hopped over me and plummeted toward the ground. Mike reached down and brushed off Aslan's fur. "Driving out here helps keep my mind off of things. I'm getting more and more concerned," he said.

Jan added, "We need to line a job up because this school is closing when the family moves to London in the fall."

"When are you going back to the States to look for a job?" asked Randy.

Mike shook the dust from his hands. "I don't know. Abdullah hasn't gotten our visas yet."

"Why don't you talk things over with him," suggested Randy. "There's time to work it out."

Mike picked up a stick and threw it. Aslan ran after it, picked it up in his mouth and stared mindlessly at Mike. "Come here, boy," Mike urged, but Aslan ran away from him, apparently engaging him in a game of chase.

Randy threw his hands into the air. "Aslan doesn't know he's a retriever!"

Hoping to keep their minds off of their problems, I suggested we explore more of the desert on foot. With the dogs following, we hiked along the desert floor and admired nature's peaceful beauty. The surrounding scenery, though, reminded me of a part of my favorite psalm I didn't usually like to think about, *walking through the valley of the shadow of death*. The words conjured up scary images and made me feel I might one day find myself walking a shaky precipice. When I glanced at the stable rock formations though, I realized that if I ever did walk through a shadowy valley, my good shepherd would be by my side, and his word would guide my faulty steps and decisions. As the sun began to set and the blue sky blended into darkening shades of indigo, we headed back and drove through the rugged terrain toward the security of our compound.

Mike suggested we invite George and Lydia to join us for dinner at a Chinese restaurant downtown. We picked them up and drove back into town. At night, the city of Riyadh came to life. Strings of bright lights hung around windows, doors and rooftops. Store windows shone brightly, revealing the goods and customers inside. The chandeliers hanging in lamp shops sparkled like desert stars in a vast moonless sky.

We parked and walked past the men's entrance of the restaurant toward the entrance we could all use, the family entrance. I was pleasantly surprised by the elegant waiting room. It was decorated with ornately carved mahogany furniture. A rock fountain gurgled softly.

The male host escorted us to the family section where the dining tables were separated by thick heavy curtains. Once we were seated and the curtains were drawn, Lydia, Jan and I shed the *abayas*, draping them carelessly over the backs of our chairs. The waiter entered between the curtains with menus and a pitcher of ice-cold water.

Mike looked fondly at his wife and said, "Jan and I wanted us to get together because we have some good news to share."

Lydia smiled at Jan and asked, "You're not pregnant, are you?"

Jan beamed. "Yes, I am. And we've waited a long time for this moment."

At last I understood Mike and Jan's heightened anxiety about going to the job fair. Their first child was on its way. Surely they wanted everything taken care of in a timely manner. We ordered some of the faux Saudi champagne made from fruit juices and bubbling mineral water and lifted our glasses to toast the happy couple.

Unfortunately, the couple's good news didn't last long. Several days later, Mike pounded wildly on our front door. When Randy opened it, Mike stormed in. "Abdullah isn't letting us out of the country."

"Can't you just book a flight and go anyway?" Randy asked.

"You can't travel without your Saudi sponsor's permission," said Mike.

"And Abdullah has all of our passports," I said slowly, regretting that we had freely turned ours over to Abdullah for 'safe keeping.'

Mike wanted to give Abdullah a piece of his mind, but Randy warned him that could mean more trouble since it seemed Abdullah had a short fuse. Mike said he'd be in trouble if he didn't have his next job lined up because he wouldn't be able to provide for his new family. He felt like he was in a no-win situation.

"Maybe George can help," suggested Randy.

"George was there the whole time, but Abdullah didn't back him or his commitment to us. I told Abdullah we only accepted his position because we were promised we could look for our next position mid-year. I told him if he didn't let us go, I'd quit, but he just sat there smugly. Your life is not your own here!"

"What about the U.S. Embassy?" I asked.

"Everyone who's lived overseas knows the embassy is worthless," Mike said sarcastically. "Abdullah is going to talk to the prince and get back to me. We are going to that job fair!"

Later that evening, Abdullah got back to Mike, but he came with an ultimatum. Mike could either apologize for insulting Abdullah with the way he talked to him, or leave the country immediately. Mike and

Jan were indignant. Without a moment's hesitation, they began packing. Abdullah gave them forty-eight hours to get organized and get out.

Neither Randy nor I could have predicted such a shocking outcome. We believed that reasoning and negotiation would have resolved the conflict. Why were educated people unable to reason? I had thought only the extremists held such primeval positions toward reasoning and negotiating. Couldn't anyone see how badly the children's education was being disrupted?

The next morning, I walked over to see Jan. A large moving van was parked in front of her home. Men from Pakistan and India were rushing back and forth, their small bodies laden with heavy boxes and tools. When I knocked on the open front door, I saw that Jan's entire place was in disarray. Packing boxes, string, tape and styrofoam pieces were scattered all about. Books were pulled off shelves and stacked in piles, pictures stood against packing boxes, clothes were piled everywhere, and Jan stood in the middle packing the crystal glasses that had been taken off of the shelves in her hutch.

"I am so mad!" She threw a cloth down on the table. "Abdullah can sure get a visa when he wants to." Jan collapsed into a chair. "Our neighbor, Bill, came over last night and said this happens all the time. I can't believe people do business like this."

I sat across from her. "Me either. Where's Mike?"

"He's at Abdullah's office getting our severance pay and passports. Then we'll fly out of here and go to the job fair. I'm going to call every recruitment agency in the States and tell them how this Abdullah guy operates! He promised us that we could go to the fairs. Mike is going to make sure Abdullah can't find teachers anywhere. I'm tired of non-professionals running schools. And how is Abdullah going to find new teachers? His search will take longer than the week we asked for. I don't know what he could possibly be thinking."

"He's not thinking logically. He just needs to save face, and he's interrupted the education of your students. Lydia and George must be pretty upset."

A loud, vigorous knock on the front door startled us. Jan motioned for her neighbor, Bill, to enter. A large man with gray hair protruding from underneath a white cowboy hat walked in. After introducing us, Jan explained the most recent events. Bill said that he had witnessed similar situations frequently in his business. Americans and Brits were hired for their professional expertise, but to correct a Saudi citizen in training could result in a loss of face and be taken as an insult. Americans were typically forced out of the country immediately so they wouldn't go through the local justice system or seek legal counsel. Traditionally, foreigners who were called *dhimmi* were not allowed access to Saudi courts. *

Bill looked sympathetically toward me. "You and your husband be careful now. There's a pattern at these small schools."

"We have a good relationship with Abdullah," I said confidently. "We've worked hard to create trust and respect." Secretly though, I was glad the contract we had signed with Abdullah in California noted that disputes would be settled amicably with three months advance notice should either side wish to terminate the agreement.

Bill sighed, "Here's my card if you need support." After promising to drop by later, he left.

Shortly afterwards, I also returned home. Within a few hours, Jan and Mike brought over a bag of leftover groceries. We stood on the porch to say good-bye. I asked for their address in the States so I'd know how they fared. Fortunately, George had written them a good letter of recommendation so they could get a good job lined up for next year.

When it was time for them to go, I embraced Jan and watched them walk toward their villa. They turned and waved solemnly. The sun was disappearing from the sky and early dusk grayed the buildings behind them. George and Lydia drove them to the airport.

Later that evening, anxiety over the Barkers' expulsion was turning my stomach into knots. I'd always expected reasonable negotiations and compromise to prevail, but they failed Mike and Jan. Neither did they have any legal recourse available to them. I went upstairs to lie down and asked God to give me his peace. Images of dark shadowy valleys seemed to control my thoughts and nothing could calm my nerves. I realized that I needed to be around friends, for comfort and support. Randy and I walked over to George and Lydia's villa, hoping George could shed some light on the situation. His experienced insight might help us prevent a conflict of our own while living in a culture where not all of the rules were obvious or explained until they were broken.

Lydia welcomed us with her usual warmth, but her face was sullen and pale. George offered us a glass of water. "Like the British doctor said when you first arrived, never back a Saudi in a corner," warned George.

"So, insulting a Saudi is cause for deportation?" Randy asked.

"Yes, but Abdullah is from Syria," said Lydia. "I've questioned where his political loyalties might be, Syria or Saudi. Saudi rulers are receptive to the West, but Syria certainly isn't. It's a known haven for some of the terrorist groups."

George said, "I think he must have been afraid to tell the prince that Mike and Jan wanted to leave again. They went to London last month for some medical tests not available in Riyadh."

Randy wondered if Mike hadn't escalated the problem, having noticed that Mike was getting fairly angry. Lydia pointed out that Mike had a good reason to be angry. Abdullah had insulted Mike by taking away his ability to provide for his own family. Besides, Abdullah got extremely hot under the collar as well.

George leaned forward and said, "Look, nobody won in this."

"The children were hurt too," said Lydia. "The disruption is devastating for their education."

I searched their eyes for understanding and asked, "Where's forgiveness in all of this?"

"Forgiveness? That's a good question," said George, shaking his head. "Akbar has mentioned that revenge is understood. In fact, it's considered justice and is expected in this culture. For instance, many people suspect that when King Faisal was assassinated in 1975, it was a revenge killing."

King Faisal had introduced many social reforms during his reign, including the opening of the first television station. The clerics initially balked at the idea of allowing television in the kingdom. When King Faisal convinced them that television could be used to spread Islam, he opened the station. Nevertheless, violent demonstrations took place around the building. One of the King's nephews, Prince Bandar ibn Musa'id, was killed when the government put down the demonstrations. Apparently, Bandar's brother, Prince Faisal, held the king responsible. During a *majlis* with a Kuwaiti delegation, young Prince Faisal snuck in as if a part of the delegation. He pulled a gun and fatally shot the king. Ten years later, the prince was publicly beheaded for assassinating the king. *

"Have you ever heard the story about the princess who was executed?" asked Lydia.

"Oh my god, no!" I gasped.

"Her name was Mishaal and her palace is not far from where your school is located. She was one of Noura's cousins."

The BBC had previously run a documentary by Thomas Sancton and Scott Macleod, which told the story of a young princess who had fallen in love with a common man. Unhappy in her arranged marriage to a much older man, she planned to flee Saudi Arabia with the young man she had fallen in love with. Her behavior greatly shamed her eldest living male relative. When he learned of the planned escape, he had the couple arrested publicly in Jeddah. She was shot as she knelt in the dirt, and nearby her lover was beheaded. * It was widely believed the 'honor killing' was a heartless act of revenge. When the documentary aired, the Saudi government threatened to throw out England's ambassador if the program was not taken off the air. The programming was suspended, but the story remained in the hearts of people.

We sat in silence, stunned by the brutality and need to save face. Discovering the depths that revenge held was disturbing. Perhaps I had taken Jesus' teachings on forgiveness for granted. His teachings were far more radical and necessary than I realized. His teachings had enabled all of us to overlook insults and the personal sacrifices we made in order to work in Saudi Arabia.

Lydia invited us to stay for dinner, but my stomach was too tense to eat. "We'll still have Thanksgiving dinner. Don't forget we want you to come," said Lydia.

Randy thanked her and rose to leave. George encouraged us to come over any time we needed to talk. We said good night and walked home holding hands. As soon as we returned, the phone rang. Randy answered it, and when he mentioned Abdullah's name, I stiffened.

After hanging up, Randy muttered, "Great. Abdullah wants to see us tomorrow morning."

"I hope we haven't insulted him. I wouldn't want to be on his bad side."

"I think we can reason with him," said Randy. "I still think Mike was too angry."

In spite of my constant prayers, I could hardly sleep that night, wondering what Abdullah wanted. I couldn't find a reprieve from the stress nor understand why my usual coping strategies weren't working. Every time I tried to meditate upon green pastures and still waters for restoration, I obsessed over the scene with Jan in her living room, fearing I could be next. The anxiety struck a familiar chord with me, but I wasn't sure why and cried out for God's comfort.

When morning came, my eyes were red and puffy. Randy drove nervously through the city and I gazed out the window thinking about Mike and Jan. How could decent and competent people experience such hardship? I longed for the peace of God that surpassed human understanding. We arrived at Abdullah's office but his door was closed. While we waited, I looked around the reception room at the tired prints hanging on the walls. The magazines were boring. The coffee was too cold to drink. Finally, Abdullah opened his door and stiffly motioned for us to enter.

"Barker insulted me," he blurted. "When he insults me, he insults

His Highness! They wanted too much time off." His fair complexion turned red.

I knew Mike and Jan's side of the story, but Abdullah intimidated me. Rationalizing that the conflict was partially Mike's fault made me feel like I could manage potential conflicts more diplomatically and not face the same unsettling fate.

Abdullah continued, "The prince told Barker that if he didn't apologize, he'd be fired." He pounded his desk with a clenched fist. "I am important!"

Glancing around his office, I saw pictures of Abdullah with this prince and that prince. The pictures convinced me that Abdullah was important. I'd always given him the benefit of the doubt, but I had never seen him behave like a tantrum-prone child, falling prey to blame and consumed with appearances. I thought he was too intelligent to succumb to such defensive behavior, or was he issuing a subtle warning to us?

Suddenly, he asked us if we would like our paychecks. I'd forgotten all about payday. It was the end of the month. A tense smile plastered his face as he handed us the ledger to sign.

"If we have any problems, we'll talk them over with you," said Randy.

"Exactly. We'll talk them over," Abdullah said, regaining a semblance of decorum.

Randy and I signed the ledger. We picked up our checks and quickly excused ourselves for work.

As Randy started the car engine he said, "The adults couldn't resolve this and they ended up hurting the children. If anything like this happens to us, we'll talk it over with him."

"And be extremely diplomatic," I added, as I lifted the black scarf over my hair.

10.

THE WRONG SIDE OF THE FENCE

FOLLOWING THE DEPORTATION of Mike and Jan, Randy and I were disheartened and disillusioned. I hoped that praying and pouring myself into my teaching would dissolve the feelings of anxiety that had surfaced during their conflict with Abdullah. And while working with Samira and Majid eventually brought some relief, the events surrounding the Barkers' expulsion were discussed for weeks. Unfortunately, the way they were expelled revealed a pattern for problem solving and a passive acquiescence to fatalism that crippled the will to intervene on behalf of justice. It also painted a picture of God as the author of evil.

Before classes began one day, a servant criticized the Barkers for wanting too much time off.

"They had an attitude," said Majid as he thumbed through a soccer magazine.

I understood Mike and Jan's perspective, but hoping to avoid the same predicament, I wanted to distance myself from people who were perceived as troublemakers. "Well, they never seemed to adjust to Saudi."

"People just come and go," sighed Majid as he nonchalantly flipped through a few more pages. "*Ensh'Allah.*"

"Yes, as God wills," repeated the loyal servant.

"I guess things work out the way they're meant," I surmised.

Samira looked at us and frowned. "But Abdullah isn't very nice to people."

I was impressed she had spoken her mind so boldly and candidly. She was the only one who didn't look at the circumstances fatalistically. Her example inspired me to be true to myself, but it also troubled me. I wondered what other incidences had led her to this conclusion. Had others met a similar fate when dealing with Abdullah?

Perhaps the 'victims' were merely insensitive invaders of an unfamiliar culture who broke protocol and brought their troubles upon themselves. Or had they broken hidden rules that no one explained? Who was really responsible for the disagreements, and who really wielded the power? Did the prince know about Abdullah's treatment of his employees? Did he condone it? I recalled how silent the family and Clarise had become when Randy and I first mentioned how we appreciated Abdullah's care and concern.

The family hired me to take care of business so they can sleep at night, Abdullah had once said when meeting with us at his office. I shuddered at his implications.

Samira and I wandered slowly upstairs to class. She seemed preoccupied, so I asked her what was on her mind.

"Abdullah ruined my cousins' school where the Barkers taught, and no one stopped him. Just because someone is having trouble doesn't mean they deserve it." She paused before admitting, "It reminds me of something my friend said about the Holocaust. There are people in my country who think the Jews deserved the Holocaust."

I was stunned, for I had never heard of such thinking. Americans had been horrified by what they saw as they liberated the people imprisoned in the German death camps at the end of World War II. Western citizens vowed never to let such atrocities occur again and felt an obligation to prevent mankind's cruelty to man by educating everyone about the horror.

"Ordinary people didn't stand up to the Germans in their madness, did they?" I asked. "Everyone played a small part and refused to look at the overriding story being played out in their own backyards. They were blind, and as a result, people's lives were utterly destroyed."

Samira continued, "Some people think the Jews did something to make God mad."

"If we think God punishes the evil and rewards the good, how do we explain that evil people seem to prosper? Or that good people seem to suffer?" An ideology that adhered to appeasing God with good works naturally causes one to think that evil is punishment for failure to do well, and I wanted Samira to think through to its logical conclusions. "Do we really believe God is the author of evil?" I asked.

"No, I hadn't looked at it like that," said Samira.

"Some of the stories in the Bible are in the *Qur'an*. Isn't Job in the *Qur'an*?" I asked.

"Yes, but it doesn't say too much about him. Just something about suffering and then getting back the things he lost," said Samira.

"If you have the chance, read the whole story of Job in the Old

Testament," I suggested.

The book of Job seemed to raise more questions than it answered about human suffering. What was interesting to me was how Job's friends responded to his plight. They accused him of doing something sinful to cause his suffering. They blamed him for his troubles. * They also suggested God was teaching him a lesson. In the beginning of the story, Job is shown as a good, upright man who loved God. Then the devil asked God if he could test Job, and God agreed. As a result, Job lost everything he valued. Job's wife told him to curse God and die. Until the end of the story, Job dutifully praised God in spite of his losses. Later, God restored everything to Job. Job's story verified the existence of evil and revealed the many different ways people responded to evil. Of course, Jesus knew suffering on the cross and showed all of humanity how to respond with forgiveness. As a result, he showed how different his nature is from ours. The book of Job also made me realize how little we understood what was happening in the spiritual realm.

"Have you heard that saying, *Evil men prosper when good men do nothing?*" I asked.

"Yes."

"God is against injustice, not the author of it. I think we have a moral duty to intervene during a time of evil. Then we'll be acting with God's heart," I suggested.

"I've been reading the autobiography of Menahem Begin's daughter because I've always wanted to know the Jew's side. I only know the Palestinian's side. And my dad is going to watch the movie called *Showa,* with Majid and me. The story about the Holocaust."

"Oh, yes, I've seen that. It's a very long documentary, but well worth seeing because they interview people who eye-witnessed the events in Germany."

"I'll let you know what I think of *Showa.*"

Samira's ability to analyze the cause and effects of events pleased me. Her willingness to look at two sides of an issue was encouraging. Whenever I witnessed my students reaching for and thinking about serious issues, teaching was rewarding. I could see Samira's potential to demonstrate caring leadership and goodness. If only her culture recognized the worth of womanhood and provided a platform for a woman's voice and perspective. Perhaps Samira could find an avenue for good within the confines of her traditions, or convince the men of her family that women could have an increasing role for good in society.

Several days later, Randy and I needed to talk with Clarise about purchasing school supplies. We knocked on her door since it was slightly ajar. She muttered something, but when we walked in, we found her crying at her desk. Embarrassed, she grabbed a tissue, dabbed at her eyes and tried to regain her composure. Our presence made me feel awkward, so I offered to come back later.

She motioned for us to enter and grabbed another tissue. When her eyes filled with tears again, she confessed, "It's Abdullah. I just hung up the phone. He's challenging every proposal and purchase I submit to him. He wants Randy to sign all of the orders I place."

"Why all the suspicion?" Randy asked.

Clarise disclosed that Abdullah had not liked the previous school administrator. She had empathized with the director, and now she suspected that Abdullah didn't like her in charge. She felt like he had been trying to force her out for some time. She hoped that if she fostered teamwork amongst the teachers, they could handle the politics and keep the school moving ahead. Clarise took a deep breath and said, "The thing is, I really like the family."

Randy said, "We know you do, because you know what Princess Noura wants. You have our support too."

Randy brought up the school's future because he wanted to encourage Clarise. He explained a proposal he planned to submit to establish a professional alliance with one of the prestigious schools the prince liked. Randy thought we should develop a relationship with a university while the children were still in high school. A university's oversight could lend credibility to our school. If the prince could fly several professors over to examine our program, they might be able to recommend the children when they apply to college.

Clarise said that if we could get that kind of credibility, it would make all of the difference. The children would be inspired to work toward excellence, the teachers would be exposed to outstanding leadership and the program was bound to improve. Everyone would benefit.

Randy said, "Abdullah didn't seem interested though. He had me write a proposal and send a few contact letters to universities. But he also told us not to mention it to Their Highnesses. We haven't heard anything from him since. Sometimes I think he simply round filed it."

I added, "He doesn't want the family to be disappointed if it doesn't work out."

Clarise said, "Frankly, Abdullah doesn't want to look bad if it falls through." She reminded us that Abdullah would have to think of Randy's proposal in light of Majid's struggles at the public school. Even though the tutors were helping him, the public school still wasn't going well. If Majid didn't find success, all of the men in his family would feel shame. Abdullah would feel ashamed if Majid was successful at the school Clarise monitored but not the school Abdullah supervised.

"Randy," she continued, "your proposals have shown me how decently you conduct business. When you first came, I thought my days were numbered."

Randy said, "I support teamwork completely, and I know the children's success will eventually transfer to their public schools and make everyone proud of Majid."

As Randy and I drove home, my thoughts turned to the haughty British doctor we had encountered when we first arrived in Riyadh. Though I'd been indignant at the comments he'd made in the restaurant, in the wake of recent events my perspective was changing.

"I'm beginning to understand where that rude British doctor was coming from," I said. "He lacked decorum, but basically, he didn't like the way his staff members were being treated. That's honorable. And I don't see any reason for Clarise to be pushed to tears or pushed out of her position. It's no wonder she was testy when we first arrived. And the Barkers . . . their situation should have been handled much more sensitively."

"I agree. I don't understand operating like this. It's destructive to both sides."

"I don't want any part of it," I said.

"And I will not end up on the wrong side of the fence. It's against everything I believe in."

The holidays of Ramadan and Christmas were approaching, and we wanted to have the next open house before the family left Riyadh for vacation in London. Unfortunately, the only day that Prince Faisal could attend an open house was Christmas Eve. Clarise worked hard to change the date because George and Lydia had invited all of the teachers to their home for Christmas dinner. Neither Clarise nor Princess Noura, however, could influence the prince to alter the date. He had worked his schedule in concordance with a number of influential princes who were coming to the palace that very evening.

Early Christmas Eve, Their Highnesses arrived at the school. The open house showcased the children's work from a unit on ancient China. To improve upon the Egyptian presentations, Majid and Samira displayed their Chinese projects in separate rooms where each could shine and be the center of attention. The art teacher, Zoe, had the children paint Asian landscapes using watercolors. In addition, Samira painted female portraits on a paper fan. Zoe framed it in a silver shadow box and hung it beside the landscapes. In English, Majid and Samira read the novel, *The Remarkable Journeys of Prince Jen,* the story of a young Chinese royal.

Prince Jen felt isolated from his kingdom because he had led a sheltered and protected life behind the walls of his ominous palace. One day he was inspired by a visiting scholar to travel to the country of Tien-ku, where it had been said a good way of life and a fair amount of happiness had been found. Along the way, Prince Jen made new friends, encountered unexpected adventures and faced numerous hardships. When he found himself condemned as a criminal and forced to wear the wooden collar, the *cangue,* about his shoulders, Prince Jen realized he had lost everything, including power, position and wealth. He learned what it meant to be a citizen of his own kingdom and discovered life's truest gifts. He found himself, made lasting friends, and fell in love with a beautiful traveling companion, Voyaging Moon. He returned to his kingdom to rule with wisdom and mercy.

Majid and Samira wrote a play based upon the travels of the Chinese prince. During their presentation, I recalled a conversation I'd had with Majid while reading *Prince Jen.*

"No one will tell the king that people in Saudi Arabia are poor," he said.

"Why?" I asked.

"Because he would get too upset. And he's already sick. Besides, in our culture, no one is supposed to bring bad news."

I watched Majid manipulate his puppet, Prince Jen, around the stage. Would Majid know what it was like to walk the poor, back streets of Saudi Arabia and feel empathy for those who experienced pain and hardship? Or would he believe suffering was their fate and allow it to continue? If only I could help Majid see the worth of a simple citizen and help him choose wisely. Like the Chinese character, would my students discover that leading a nation wisely was more important than leading a good life of fame and riches, sports cars and haute couture, horse races and diamond studded jewels?

Clarise approached me while we were watching the performance. "You've made learning a joy for them, Kristin. This is what happens when teachers respect their students and build self-esteem."

I was deeply pleased to receive Clarise's heartfelt approval. Together we had established a safe place where the children could question, learn and flourish. Our growing camaraderie and common goals benefited the children. The present success made the challenge of overcoming my differences with Clarise well worth any perceived slight on my part.

After the play, Prince Faisal wished the teachers a Merry Christmas. I appreciated his acknowledgement of the Christian holiday. Princess Noura joined us and said how pleased she was with the children's work. She reminded us that she'd like the children to have several weeks of additional classes during Ramadan. We agreed to her request. The prince and princess thanked the teachers and returned to the palace with Majid and Samira following cheerfully behind them.

While the staff members cleaned up, Abdullah told Randy he'd like to talk with the teachers. Shortly, we gathered in the lobby.

Abdullah cleared his throat and said, "There's a word of caution I need to add. The students you're teaching are royal students, so you should not become too close to them. This is the only school Majid cares about. He'd rather spend all of his time here. They should be successful at both schools."

Randy explained, "With only one student in the class at a time, we can give Majid more attention than a public school teacher can. He simply feels successful here."

I felt badly that Abdullah was anxious and said, "The success Majid achieves here will transfer to his other school."

Ignoring my comment, Abdullah repeated, "The teachers shouldn't become too close."

"The relationships are quite normal, I assure you," said Clarise in defense of her staff.

"I need to attend to the prince, so if you will, excuse me." Abdullah turned abruptly and headed out the door.

Once Abdullah was gone, Clarise said, "I don't understand him. When I first arrived, the princess wanted me to be close with the children. Now Abdullah's saying the opposite."

Randy said, "The princess knows what she wants. He should just listen to her."

Clarise collapsed into one of the nearby chairs. "The princess is very pleased with our school, and this is the one that matters to her. I overheard Noura saying that she didn't care if the kids got D's in the public school, but I also overheard Majid having a big argument with the religion tutor. Their voices got very loud. Abdullah's probably stressed about the public school. I wonder just what goes on over there." She promised she'd keep the princess informed about our school.

Randy added, "Let's just hope that Faisal's father doesn't find out about this school, or all of our jobs could be in jeopardy."

"Don't worry. Noura and Faisal are committed to this school," said Clarise. "And besides, Faisal's father simply wants his grandchildren to be in touch with the people. I know you understand that."

And it was true. What good was a leader who didn't know the people of his country?

Zoe was eager to get Christmas festivities underway and said she'd see everyone at George and Lydia's. We decided to close up school and begin the holiday celebrations.

On the way to George and Lydia's Randy said, "In class the other day Majid said Abdullah tried to tell Prince Faisal we were too close to the children."

"What did the prince say?" I asked.

"He said the relationships were just right. Majid said Abdullah's face turned bright red when the prince disagreed."

"Do you think he's jealous?"

Randy shook his head. "Majid thought so, but how could he be?"

"If the prince thinks everything is alright, then we don't have anything to worry about." In his position of power, he would be able to take care of anything that arose.

When we drove onto our compound, we passed several villas trimmed with Christmas lights. Other homes had brightly decorated Christmas trees in the windows. Since the displays were considered anti-Islamic, these were the only decorations that I'd seen anywhere in Riyadh. A few carolers strolled along the lanes with choir books in hand. Glad to see Westerners keeping some holiday traditions, I waved at them.

Once we arrived, Lydia greeted us and led us into the living room.

Zoe's husband, Brian, chided us. "Working on Christmas Eve! What's wrong with you two?"

"The family's been good to us, so we don't mind doing something for them," said Randy.

Clarise arrived next and quickly inquired about Mike and Jan. While pouring her drink, George told us that they had accepted a position in Bangladesh for next year. I was relieved that they had attended the international job fairs after all. I had worried about them, and no one was saying anything kind about them. George admitted that they were being badmouthed at his school too. "And they were such good teachers," he sighed.

"And now they're evil people who deserved their fate," noted Randy sadly.

Clarise said, "I wanted to thank you for your support at the school, Randy and Kris."

"Of course," I said smiling.

Lydia escorted an unfamiliar couple into the living room. "I'd like everyone to meet Mohammed and Anna Habib. They teach at the British school."

We had heard great things about the British school. Mohammed and Anna related that they were happy there because the class size was low and the pay was good. Over the years, they had traveled the world teaching in different British schools.

When Clarise asked what we'd all be doing over Ramadan, I had to admit that the only thing I knew about Ramadan was that it lasted forty days. Clarise explained that it honored the time when Mohammed received the *Qur'an* through revelation. During the day, Muslims prayed and fasted, abstaining from water and food. Usually during the day they slept. After sunset, families gathered to break their fast with a time of great feasting. The celebrating often lasted through the night. Normal schedules and routines were essentially reversed.

Clarise continued, "Their Highnesses will fly to their home in London. I'll be flying with them because my mother has a vacation home there also. I'm going to visit with her and do some shopping."

Anna said, "The weather is so lovely this time of year, I think we'll stay here, play a lot of tennis and rest beside the pool."

Mohammed protested, saying that the entire city would close down and resemble a ghost town. People would either be sleeping during the day or out of the country. Foreigners who stayed in Riyadh wouldn't be able to carry on daily business because nothing would be open. The grocery stores, the banks, and the streets would be virtually empty, and the malls would be closed. If people were in a restaurant and caught eating or drinking in public, they could be thrown in jail or beaten. He encouraged Anna to think about leaving town for the holidays.

Lydia said, "We've stayed here during Ramadan and regretted it, so we're taking a train ride through India. It follows an old palace route," said Lydia.

"Maybe we can do that sometime," I said, glancing hopefully at Randy.

Randy cringed and said, "I hate to spend money though. We're trying to clear debt."

George suggested that we drive to Bahrain, the island nation in the Persian Gulf. Bahrain was predominantly a Muslim country, but had centuries of exposure to both Western and Eastern cultures, its coastal location placing it near historic trade routes. Both the Portuguese and the British had established control over the nation for the purposes of colonization and trade. Later, the prominent Al-Khalifah family, who fled the aggressive Wahabbi warriors of Abdul Aziz, found safety on the gulf island. They established their rule, and the austere Wahabbism never took root. Men and women were allowed in theaters, malls and restaurants together. Women were allowed to drive, and Western women weren't required to cover. The relaxed and tolerant environment was the only motivation I needed to persuade my husband to visit Bahrain.

Randy smiled and said, "Frankly, I'm getting real tired of driving you around every time you want to go somewhere. Whoever decided women couldn't drive created headaches for men."

Clarise advised us to notify Abdullah so he could process our visas and retain our house keys. He would also need to request permission for our travels from Princess Noura. Foreigners were not allowed to travel in the kingdom without official permission.

Mohammed and Anna decided to go to Bahrain and offered to show us around. They knew where the good restaurants and nightclubs were in Manama, the capital city. When George and Lydia wrote out the directions for us, I realized the trip would be like the four-hour drive from Los Angeles to Las Vegas. It seemed like a very manageable and affordable excursion if we could find someone to care for our dogs.

Finally, Lydia announced that dinner was ready. The aromas of her roast turkey, gravy, potatoes and dressing wafted through the air. Cranberry sauce, pumpkin pie and coffee were set on a small dessert table. She directed us to a festive dining table that was set with a red jacquard tablecloth and white china. In the center were fresh red roses in a silver vase. George showed us where to sit and led us in a blessing acknowledging the birth of our dear Savior and thanking God for friendships that had been forged on the other side of the world. We sang S*ilent Night,* a cappella, and I felt the presence of the Lord among us.

I missed Mike and Jan and asked God to help them find kindness and fulfillment in their next position. It seemed like the four of us had just been shopping, dining and exploring the wonders of the desert, and suddenly they were gone. I didn't want to be governed by a sense of fatalism that allowed injustice to be perpetuated in the name of God. I also hoped I'd be able to stay positive about my surroundings and believe the best in people, but since the Barker's lives had been so callously interrupted, I wondered if staying too positive would naively cause me to close my eyes to tragic conditions that affected the lives of people from around the world who came to work in Saudi Arabia. If it did, it could also keep me from caring about them.

11.

SEARCHED

SEVERAL DAYS LATER, Randy and I started across the Arabian Peninsula toward Bahrain. I was looking forward to a much-deserved rest and a taste of freedom. Just outside of Riyadh, we passed the camel *souk*. Miles of canvas tents stretched across the desert sands amidst wooden posts and wire corrals. Rocks and tumbleweeds dotted the landscape amongst the corrals. Camels, along with their babies, grazed lazily at their food troughs. An hour later, we passed a camel herd grazing on the sparse grass. Randy stopped the car so I could take some pictures.

He joined me beside the fence. "I wonder if that story about the Pakistani shepherd is true."

"Which one was that?" I asked, looking through the viewfinder.

"Remember the guy who was dropped off in the middle of the desert?"

"No," I said, clicking the shutter button. The camel lifted its neck and snorted.

"His Saudi sponsor blindfolded him for the drive and left him with a camel herd. Workers dropped off food every month and sped away so he couldn't hop onto the truck."

Apparently the shepherd died when the cold weather hit, but the sponsor's behavior was so reprehensible, I could hardly believe the story. Of course, I couldn't believe slavery was legal until 1962 either. I put the camera away and said, "I get tired of this victim stuff."

"Maybe people make these stories up to make Saudis look bad."

"Who told you about it anyway?" I asked as we returned to the car.

"Seid. He knows all the Pakistani and Indian workers living on the compound."

"Well, if it is true, it's a tragedy."

Further down the highway, the rocks disappeared from the terrain and the smooth sand glistened under the sun. Randy parked along the side of the road again so we could explore the dunes. I took off my shoes and we ran to the top of one dune and then down the backside where we saw one wave of rippling, ruddy sand dune after another. Occasional wisps of weeds protruded from the sandy drifts. I was taking photos of the rust-colored mounds and distant camel herds when Randy slipped up behind me and enfolded me in his embrace. "Have you noticed anything different out here?"

I turned around. "The sand seems to go on forever, and the sky, well it's simply beautiful." Suddenly, a sweet, alluring smile emerged on his face.

"No, we're alone under God's big blue sky." He nuzzled my ear with his lips. After a lingering, romantic interlude, we sorted our belongings, grabbed the *abaya* and trudged back to the car. Once on our way, we plugged a rock and roll tape into the stereo, turned the volume up as loud as we could, and sang our way to the border.

We reached the Gulf and drove over the bridge that connected the Arabian Peninsula with the island nation of Bahrain. The lines of cars leaving Saudi seemed endless as they vied for a position close to the officials checking exit visas and stamping passports. Crossing the border was nerve-wracking. Unsure about procedures and policies, we handed the guard everything in our possession. We let him select the papers he needed. The guard smiled, stamped our passports and waved us on. We followed George's directions to an upscale hotel in downtown Manama. Since we were tired from the drive, we ate and fell fast asleep.

When the sun rose the next morning, we realized that we had an expansive view of the north end of the island. Beyond a modern skyline of towering high rises were the sparkling waters of the Persian Gulf. The blue waves shimmered and danced as if a multitude of diamonds had been cast over them. An immense mosque stood on the nearby shores. Its stately minarets rose gracefully into the blue sky. Verdant palm groves dotted the island under a pale blue sky. I wondered if Bahrain had really been the site of the Garden of Eden as some archaeologists claimed. Whatever it was historically, it was now an oasis of freedom and rest for us. Just gazing over the expanse of the island and ocean lifted my spirits.

After breakfast, we took a cab to the local museum. It was closed, so the cab driver gave us a private tour of the island, promising to show us places that tourists usually didn't see. First, we stopped at the home of an old weaver. His home was a simple, gray wooden shack with cracks between the slats. A Persian rug covered the dirt floor. The windows were covered with fabric that flapped in the breeze. Outside, a tiny old man was weaving a bolt of *abaya* fabric as his fathers had before him. The loom stretched across the sand for about twenty-five feet. Amongst strands of black thread, he wove a geometric pattern with red thread. It would take him several months to finish the bolt.

Next, the cab driver took us into a poor section of the island located amongst ancient burial grounds. The huge mounds of dirt rose amongst the sands, and dirt roads wound around them. Posters of a popular Iranian religious leader were plastered on walls and buildings everywhere. Graffiti filled every blank space. We asked the driver to translate the Farsi for us, and he replied that the writing expressed the people's dissatisfaction with Bahrain's current government. They believed the emir to be a rich playboy influenced by Western decadence and ignorant of the needs of the poor. Looking around at their wretched living conditions, it was difficult to offer any defense for the lavish, extravagant lifestyle of the rich.

The driver looked at us through the rearview mirror. "You Americans are different from the British. The British were here for many years. And when they come, they bring their tea sets and tables and set them up under a pavilion a long distance from us, the people of Bahrain. But you Americans, you join us on our blankets under the palm trees, drink our tea and coffee and try to understand us. You eat with us and talk with us. This is why we like you."

"Thank you," I said. "We enjoy learning about other places and people."

Amongst the sandy burial mounds was a pottery business run by gifted artisans. They were making pottery much the same way as their ancestors had for centuries. On one mound of dirt stood several large vats where the clay was softened and mixed by stomping. Inside a dilapidated slat-wood building, several small-framed men were shaping clay on old wooden potter's wheels that they controlled using foot pedals. In another room, men were carving intricate geometric designs on vases and pots. An enormous kiln stood on a dirt mound outside, where the pieces were baked. After the pots and vases cooled, the workers brushed them free of debris. Some of the pottery was painted and polished. Finally all of the vases, pots and candleholders were placed in a large room that served as a store and was open to the public. Randy and I bought several vases to remember the people of the island by.

Later that evening we met Mohammed and Anna in our hotel lobby. Unfortunately, they were extremely distressed. "We've had a terrible time," said Mohammed indignantly.

"What happened?" I asked.

Anna's eyes clouded over with tears as Mohammed explained a nasty encounter. When their cab stopped in front of their hotel, Mohammed leaned over to pick up some packages. Anna stepped onto the curb first and a Saudi man standing on the sidewalk began feeling her.

Anna's tears spilled over the rims of her eyes. "It was broad daylight, and Mohammed was right there. I slapped the guy in the face as hard as I could."

Mohammed continued, "The guy slapped her back so hard she fell onto the pavement. I was furious! When I got out of the cab, I lunged at him slugging with both fists. A security guard had to come and break it up, but he just let the Saudi go. I marched into the hotel to file a complaint, but the manager defended the Saudi, saying that the man thought my wife was a prostitute!"

"I have never been so humiliated," whispered Anna.

"No one apologized. There was absolutely no justice. We checked out immediately," said Mohammed. "We will never, never stay there again."

Since both Mohammed and Anna wanted to put the event behind them, we decided we needed a safe place to relax. Our hotel had been comfortable, so we suggested having dinner there and hoped that Anna and Mohammed would feel better after being around friends.

After dinner, we drove to the mall where the movie theater was. We saw an American movie, but what struck me about the film was the high level of violence, emotionally traumatizing events and vile language. I wondered if such movies didn't portray an inaccurate view of America to the world? I also prayed the movie wouldn't upset Anna any further. Soon we said good night and wished Anna and Mohammed better luck in their new hotel. I told Anna if she needed to talk to someone, to please call me.

The next day, Randy and I went to the gold *souk* where we purchased 21-karat gold earrings for friends in America. We soon found ourselves wandering the back streets where no tourists seemed to be. Several shopkeepers yelled out and beckoned us to do business with them, and some leered at my uncovered blonde hair. I ignored them and held onto Randy. One older and heavier woman walked by surveying me up and down with blatant disapproval. Her scolding stare made me wonder what she thought about Western women. Since I was becoming anxious, we turned down an alley that led us back to the tourist section and took a cab to our hotel.

Our brief encounter with freedom was drawing to a close. We packed and drove toward the Saudi customs check. Having passed through once before, we waited patiently in line. Finally, the guard motioned for Randy to pull into the next space. Like other travelers, we got out to wait for the inspector.

This time we had our papers and passports organized and handed them confidently to the guard. Frowning, he thumbed through them and pointed for us to stand aside. He opened the door on the driver's side, ran his hands under the dashboard, searched under the front seats. He opened the trunk and lifted the upholstered flooring, searching every inch. I was annoyed when the guard removed the divider that separated the back seat from the trunk. Randy and I glanced around at other travelers. They weren't being searched like we were. They were being cleared to the next stop. The guard then opened the back doors, pulled up the entire seat and ran his hands under the cushions and along the sides.

Randy was irritated and peered over his shoulder. "What is he looking for?"

I glanced at the customs re-entry card in my hands and saw the bold-faced red letters saying, *Drug smuggling is punishable by death.* My heart beat faster. Realizing how vulnerable we were, I grabbed Randy's arm and whispered, "Oh my god, what if something was planted on our car while we were parked at the hotel or mall." I pointed to the warning. "Did you see this?"

"Yeah, I remember reading it when we flew into Riyadh last fall."

The guard moved over to the front passenger seat and noticed my black purse that I had left there. I was appalled when he picked it up without permission and yanked the zipper to open it.

"You won't find anything!" I snapped. Without a word, he carelessly tossed my purse back onto the seat. Everything fell out and lay scattered about the passenger seat and floor. The guard returned to the trunk and slammed it shut. Walking sternly toward a small station, he stamped our passports and handed them coldly to Randy. He motioned to Randy to get in and leave. With a huge sigh of relief, we got into the car and sped away. I picked up the items lying on the floor and put them back into my purse.

Randy looked into his rearview mirror. "What do we look like, criminals?" he asked sarcastically.

"I bet he was looking for drugs."

"He probably thinks everyone in the West does drugs."

The remainder of our ride was quiet and subdued. We had five more police checks to cross on our way into Riyadh, but fortunately no one searched us like we had been at the border. When we returned to the safety and familiarity of our compound, we were greatly relieved to see other Americans, Brits and Australians going calmly about their business.

There were still several weeks before classes resumed, and I meditated on Psalm Twenty-three, choosing to focus on the verse that the Lord was my shepherd and I need not want. I struggled to regain a sense of security after the invasive search, but unfortunately, the invasion triggered my anxiety just the way the trip to the mall had done when we first arrived in Saudi and had encountered the religious police. Though I longed for God's peace, I wondered if God wanted me to experience discomfort. Perhaps he was stirring up a sense of outrage over the injustices I had been exposed to. Perhaps I was creating a false sense of security that left me in darkness, and perhaps I shouldn't fear the discomfort. Clearly there were those who didn't want Americans in Saudi Arabia, and clearly people were suffering at their hands.

12.

REVENGE TAKES A PAWN

WHEN RAMADAN ENDED, classes resumed. We saw smiling faces again and learned that everyone had a relaxing vacation. Clarise had yet to return from England, but we expected her any day. We plunged into our next unit of study, European Medieval and Renaissance times. In English, Majid and Samira read an abridged edition of *Hamlet*, Shakespeare's story about the Danish prince who sought to uncover the reason for the mysterious and untimely death of his father, the King of Denmark. After completing the story, Majid and I had a challenging discussion about revenge. His response caught me off guard but provided much needed insight into the way problems were often solved throughout the Middle East.

Looking at me as if I were the student, Majid declared, "Of course Hamlet was justified in taking revenge for his father's death."

I had such deep beliefs about the immorality of revenge; I couldn't believe what I'd heard.

Majid sat up straight. "He *had* to get revenge for his father's death."

"Well, how do we know for certain that the king was murdered by his own brother?"

"The ghost wandering the castle told Hamlet." Majid began tapping his pencil on the desk.

"How do we know the ghost was honest?"

"I believe in ghosts."

"I believe in spiritual beings too, but what if this ghost was evil? And what if Hamlet's own heart was twisted so he only saw and heard what he wanted?"

"But Hamlet proved his uncle was guilty when he gave the play for him. Remember how Hamlet's uncle reacted?"

I nodded, recalling the uncle's apparent alarm.

"That proved he was guilty," said Majid. "Hamlet didn't even need the ghost."

"That's a good point, because it convinced Hamlet. But was Hamlet interpreting the reaction accurately? Should that convince the readers of the uncle's guilt? And where's the real evidence? Was Hamlet above the law? Maybe Hamlet's interpretation revealed a flaw in his own character."

Majid fidgeted nervously in his chair. "The uncle was guilty. He just wanted to be king."

I noticed Majid's growing discomfort and told him it was perfectly fine to disagree with one another without losing respect for each other. We were merely exploring interpretations and looking for lessons we could learn about human nature from Hamlet's story. Majid relaxed.

"Let's say, for argument's sake, that the ghost told the truth, and the uncle killed Hamlet's father. Didn't Hamlet pay a heavy price for taking revenge?" I asked.

"He had to do it for his father's honor," Majid insisted. "And maybe he was being just. He was a prince."

"Good point. Some believe Hamlet was seeking a kind of social justice. But does revenge ever honor anyone's memory? And was taking revenge worth the price he paid in the end? Everyone important in Elsinore died because of it. Doesn't Hamlet share the guilt for its total destruction?"

Majid was silent.

"Hamlet makes us ask how we should respond to evil," I said. "Is revenge our only choice? What about forgiveness, or the rule of law? Is a leader, even if he is a prince, 'above the law?'"

"When can we see the video?" he asked. "I want to see the one where Mel Gibson plays Hamlet."

I sighed with frustration. "We can see it tomorrow since it's the last day of the week. And I want you to pay attention to the price Hamlet paid for his revenge. It destroyed everything precious to him. Shakespeare was challenging us to think about the consequences of revenge, and today his words encourage us not to become its pawns. There must be other ways to solve problems."

I asked Majid if he had heard anything about Clarise. He thought she was sick and was recuperating somewhere in Spain. As he left, I felt a wave of fatigue, so I collapsed into my chair. I was ruminating over my conversation with Majid about Prince Hamlet when I heard a knock on my classroom door. Startled, I jumped in the chair.

"Sorry I spooked you," Randy apologized, as he entered and sat in Majid's chair.

Relieved to see him I said, "I was immersed in the quagmire of medieval intrigue and the flaws of human nature."

"Fun! Are the materials Clarise ordered working?" He took a spin in the swivel chair, and I rolled my eyes at my husband's boyish antics.

"Oh, yes, she did a great job, but Majid and I are having quite a discussion about revenge. I'm developing a new appreciation for the way Shakespeare challenged Western thinking."

"We're studying *The Prince* by Machiavelli, and that's intriguing," said Randy.

"I'll bet," I said. "Is he really as ruthless and cold-hearted as he's represented?"

"I think so because Machiavelli didn't believe a prince needed to follow traditional morality in order to preserve his power. He thought the appearance of virtue was fine if it served the prince's purpose, but the practice of virtue was not necessary. He said it was better for a prince to be feared rather than loved."

"What did Majid say about that?"

"He could understand Machiavelli's point because the goal was to preserve the state. Majid also said his relatives admit the expansion of Islam occurred through military conquest but believed in the end Islam was good for the people."

"Who did Machiavelli think the state was for, the citizens or the prince?" I asked.

"That's the question, isn't it?" Randy said.

Randy went on to explain that Machiavelli portrayed a low view of the common person, with little value other than to make a prince feel important and maintain his power. In *The Prince,* there wasn't any concept of 'unalienable rights' for the people like the British philosopher, John Locke, advocated. We realized that Locke's view of a republic developed later in time, and that Machiavelli addressed his views of a republic in other writings. *The Prince,* however, provided a cold, calculating prescription for obtaining and keeping political power.

I said, "If you are a person of faith and in leadership, you need to ask yourself why God has placed you in a position of power. Is it for you, or is to care for the people? If a person's answer is to care for God's people, Machiavelli is a snake, and his insidious ways a path to destruction for everyone including the state."

"I agree," said Randy. "Every leader is accountable to someone, be it God or the people, for his behavior. A prince, or president, might think he's above the law, or is the law himself, but his morality affects his judgment and therefore the welfare of every member of his kingdom."

The next day, we arrived at the palace to watch *Hamlet* in the family's private theater. Since Majid was fascinated with the way other royals lived, I hoped that watching the video would help him think about the consequences of pursuing revenge. Though the video was long, Majid was enchanted. He followed the story carefully until the final sword scene. As soon as it became clear that Hamlet was a tarnished hero who would pay for his revenge with his life, Majid got up from his chair. He walked over to his game station, turned it on and ordered a servant to bring him his newest video game.

"Majid," I whispered. "Majid, the movie isn't over yet."

He shrugged his shoulders. I didn't know how to make a prince cooperate when he was determined not to, but Majid saw that Hamlet paid heavily for his revenge and that it produced no victors. I hoped he would remember Hamlet's plight and choose more wisely than Hamlet in his own life, and leave the wiles of Machiavelli for fools.

The next week a heavy rainstorm hit Riyadh. Randy and I discovered that our regular route to work was blocked by floods. We found an alternate route and eventually made it to school.

During English, Majid was unusually restless. Finally he blurted, "Clarise's friend threatened to blow up a plane if he didn't get a million dollars from the Saudi he works for."

Recalling the flurry of rumors that circulated when Mike and Jan left, I knew better, and told him that didn't sound like the Clarise I knew.

"Well, she's being investigated, so she's not coming back." He studied his hands and then glanced out of the window at the rain that slid slowly down the pane.

"But she loves it here," I protested.

He stared at the desk. "We . . . they think she's working with a terrorist who wants to overthrow our family. Maybe she has a dark side."

"Majid, I think we all have a dark side somewhere, but Clarise loves you guys. I'm sure of that, and I know that would outweigh anything else."

He shook his head sadly. "So many people leave and never come back."

My heart went out to him. Clarise had worked for his family for nearly three years, and I knew he depended upon her. Surely he felt let down. Though Majid had to prepare for an exam on Hamlet, neither of us could concentrate on the review lesson. Who was this evil friend of Clarise's? What would happen if Clarise couldn't keep the princess informed about the school? And most importantly, would the person who took her place be able to provide the same quality of support and communication?

Over the course of the following month, I worried constantly about Clarise. Her concern for Majid and Samira was unmatched, and her absence was devastating not only to the school, but to all of us involved with the school. When she called our home I was relieved to hear from her but also troubled with her news. While visiting her mother in London, her fiancé had been falsely accused of threatening to blow up a plane unless he received a million dollars. Clarise was devastated when he'd been confronted by FBI agents in New York. Agents called her in London with fearsome questions and she felt at a loss to help Hunter. She explained that she was not being allowed to return to Saudi Arabia in spite of interventions by the Princess. She asked me if I could gather her personal belongings still in her villa on the palace grounds. I assured Clarise that I would do everything possible to send her belongings to London. I prayed that somehow she'd be allowed to return to Saudi, but my hopes were dashed when Abdullah hired a replacement for Clarise.

At home, Randy flipped through the pages of the replacement's resume. Abdullah had asked Randy to look over a resume for a Sylvia Vanderhort, but apparently Abdullah had never checked her background.

Randy said, "I don't feel good about this candidate after reading her resume. One year here, another there. There are irregularities with short-term employment and a demotion too. It makes her look unstable . . . like she can't get along with anyone. I'd never have hired someone with a record like this."

"I can't imagine Abdullah would hire someone for the royal family without checking their background. You'd better check her references, or our school could be in trouble."

Randy checked the resume again. Her last position was in Johannesburg, South Africa, so he decided to contact the school's administration. He called directory assistance in Johannesburg, but the school wasn't listed. When he couldn't find the school, he wondered if the name had been intentionally changed to hide some kind of a problem. We knew a woman on the compound who was from Johannesburg and contacted her in case she might be familiar with the schools. Indeed, she knew about the school, but said the name on the resume was incomplete and gave Randy the correct name. With the right information, Randy secured the number of the school and contacted the supervisor.

After a lengthy conversation, Randy hung up the phone. "No wonder the name of the school was wrong. I'll bet this Sylvia didn't want us to contact it. You won't believe what the supervisor said about her."

"I've got a pretty good idea from the look on your face."

"First, the supervisor apologized for giving a negative evaluation, but he wanted to protect our school from going through the trouble his school did when she worked for him."

My eyes widened and my curiosity piqued. Randy paced the floor and related that apparently the woman was a troublemaker. She didn't respect the supervisor's authority, so the school board said her contract wouldn't be renewed. She immediately left the country under false pretenses and never returned to finish her contract.

"At least you've saved the school some trouble. Why didn't Abdullah find this out?"

"He hired her because she had gray hair. It's a cultural value to respect elders, but I'm sure tired of doing his homework." Randy collapsed on the couch and threw the resume on the floor.

I knew I could never work for someone with a reputation like that. We didn't know what we were going to do with the information. On one hand, we didn't want to upset Abdullah, but on the other hand, Majid and Samira deserved a principal with a better performance record.

I threw my hands into the air. "We're always between a rock and a hard place! Why do we always have to make choices like this?"

"The princess and the children come first. I can't in good conscience support this woman. I'll write a memo to Abdullah and tell him what I found out. I guess it's not his fault since the name of the school in Johannesburg was wrong. It was difficult to get through. We'll help him smooth it over somehow."

"You don't miss a trick, honey. I'm proud of you."

Randy faxed a memo to Abdullah, and within minutes Abdullah called. He asked us to stop by his office on our way into work. Anxious about another meeting, Randy and I prayed together for God's wisdom and words.

It rained again the next morning. We drove along flooded streets to Abdullah's office and waited quietly in the reception room. We were anxious to discuss the new information and explore solutions, but when Abdullah opened the door, his face was grave and sullen.

His eye twitched and he avoided looking us in the eyes. He motioned for us to have a seat. After the usual exchange of polite greetings and small talk, Randy brought up Clarise's replacement. He was glad he'd checked the references before Miss Vanderhort actually arrived in Saudi Arabia.

Abdullah took a deep breath. "Well, I can just hear the prince speaking to me now." He stared blankly into the distance and verbalized an imagined conversation between himself and the prince. "'Abdullah, how could you recommend this person to me? Are you a child?'"

Abdullah sat quietly for a moment, looking extremely depressed. Though Prince Faisal struck me as a gracious and understanding employer, I realized that Abdullah must either fear him or fear losing face. Abdullah's psychological journey to shame appeared quickly traveled.

Randy said, "The application had misleading information. The prince can't blame you for that. Since we understand this paper process, we can help explain what happened."

Abdullah paused for a moment. "By the way, will you be returning to the school next fall?"

Randy nodded. "Of course. We love this job."

Silence flooded the room like the rain outside was flooding the streets. Abdullah's countenance transformed completely. His depression masked with a foreboding, dark demeanor, he finally said, "Randy, we won't need you as a director next year."

While Randy showed no emotion, the color drained from his face. "I never cared about being a director. It was your idea from the beginning."

He leaned forward. "Yes, well, I have some other news. The American professors we've contacted have agreed to come and evaluate the school. The prince will fly them over in a couple of weeks. We have time to prepare for their visit."

Randy spoke stiffly. "Good. I'm glad you pursued this. I want to stay involved."

Though bewildered by the turn of events and caught off guard, I forced myself to be positive. "I've been looking forward to their visit for a long time. We have many questions for them."

Abdullah picked up some papers and coldly handed them to Randy. "We'll have our first meeting three weeks from Saturday. Here's the agenda. Would you meet them at the airport?" Abdullah sat back in his chair with an air of condescension. "And, Randy, since you write so well, would you fax them the agenda?"

"Fine." Randy rose and headed toward the door. "And remember, I'll be glad to explain how difficult it was to contact Vanderhort's references."

Abdullah simply nodded and turned his back on us under the guise of rummaging through his file cabinet.

We murmured good-bye and left promptly for work. At least the professors were coming, and I congratulated Randy for his diligence. We decided to focus on the upcoming meeting with the university professors because they were the best in their fields and would help us move the school forward. In time, I hoped Abdullah would overcome his moodiness. Though I was relieved that Randy had protected the children from a potential troublemaker, I was at a loss to explain his demotion. Fortunately, Randy didn't really care whether he was a director or not, but it meant something to Abdullah.

13.

SHIFTING SANDS

SINCE THE AMERICAN professors would be arriving in Riyadh soon, Randy, the children and I spent the next several weeks preparing. We arranged everything like we had for the open houses on ancient Egypt and ancient China. Majid and Samira rehearsed their presentations once again. As we watched them, we noted their tremendous growth and were beaming with pride. Unfortunately, we weren't able to prepare for all of the events or predict the intrigue that would transpire.

As soon as the professors had settled into their hotel, they toured the school. They studied the children's assignments and listened intently to their presentations. Afterwards, the teachers met with the professors. George and Abdullah joined us. Abdullah opened the meeting by welcoming the three distinguished educators, Dr. James, Dr. Gelt and Dr. Oman, each one representing a prestigious Ivy League school that the prince respected.

Randy addressed the prince's guests. "We're honored to meet you and are most pleased that we can discuss the school's future with such great experts."

I proudly added, "My husband began planning this conference last fall, so needless to say, I'm excited we've reached this point."

Abdullah abruptly interrupted me saying, "Prince Faisal."

Randy looked up from his agenda. "Excuse me?"

"This was Prince Faisal's idea."

"Not really," said Randy.

Abdullah stiffened; his face turned red. "This was the prince's idea."

Randy said, "The prince made it clear that he wanted his children to go to a prestigious college. But, it was my idea to establish a connection with a university ahead of admissions."

Abdullah repeated himself like a broken record. "This was the prince's idea."

I was embarrassed and puzzled by Abdullah's public contradiction of my husband. Why did Abdullah feel at liberty to humiliate us in front of such revered peers?

Clearly annoyed, Randy frowned. "Whatever. Let's move along."

He addressed the professors again and mentioned how much we had been looking forward to their visit. They asked to begin our discussion with the children's work samples. Dr. Gelt said that the projects were interesting, but he thought we could be more rigorous with grading. Randy explained that we graded high intentionally, so the students would feel encouraged. We knew they had missed some of their schooling due to the Gulf War and certain royal obligations. Though we had always followed a state-approved curriculum, all of the teachers agreed to grade the students against themselves.

The only female professor, Dr. James said, "On the other hand, you have a wonderful thing going on here. You could do away with grading altogether. Just prepare the kids for testing and play the standardized test game when it comes to college admissions."

Randy replied, "That would work nicely. One of the things we're concerned about though is which school should count as credit when applying for college admissions, their Saudi public school, or their American program. The children study all through the day, and we'd like to ensure the best use of their time." Randy made an additional suggestion. "When you meet with the parents, perhaps you can help them decide which program they want to emphasize."

"We'll try to address that issue," said Dr. Gelt.

Pulling out a professional manual, Dr. James flipped through the pages. "There's another thing we'd like to discuss. Let's examine the relationships you have with Majid and Samira."

Abdullah's sullen expression changed and he looked on with heightened interest.

Dr. Oman said, "Because the students are royal, you shouldn't be too close to them."

Randy frowned. "This has been mentioned before, but I don't think it's a problem."

I still wasn't sure exactly what was meant by this comment, and I felt awkward explaining myself in an area where I had experienced affirmation from supervisors in the past. I also was confident that Clarise had modeled professional behavior for us.

Dr. James politely handed us a manual that had a model for teacher-student relationships.

"In the Muslim school room," said Dr. Oman, "the children show respect for the teachers."

Since we felt respected by our students, I wondered if he was referring to something that had a different cultural definition than what we were accustomed to. If not, I had no idea what he meant.

Abdullah sat back in his chair. An arrogant smile crossed his face. Randy reached for the book and asked to read it. We glanced over the model in the handbook together.

Randy said, "But this describes precisely the relationship we have with the students."

Dr. Oman protested, "But your students are royal. When you sit around the table for lunch, it's like you two are mom and pop, and the prince and princess are your kids."

Stunned by the analogy, I explained, "We respect our students, and they respect us."

Randy pointed to a column in the professor's manual. "And it says right here that one of the best indicators of a child's future success is his or her positive relationship with a mentor."

Abdullah interjected sternly, "And that mentor would be me."

His statement was a clear indication of his envy, but I also knew that Abdullah spent all of his time either in his office or at George's school with the cousins. And while Majid and Samira were consistently polite to him, they were not fond of him. In fact, Samira despised him and the way he treated people.

Professor James recommended that Abdullah watch a movie about a U.S. Marine who became an inner city teacher and had many obstacles to overcome before learning could transpire. One of the first things the teacher did was to establish mutual trust and respect and a healthy rapport with her students. As soon as the students learned to trust the teacher and understood that she cared about them, the students surpassed all expectations in their studies of literature. Their accomplishments were commendable. Dr. James thought viewing the movie would help Abdullah understand where Randy and I were coming from and the type of vision we had for Majid and Samira. I thought it interesting that Dr. James and Clarise had made the same connection between the learning styles of the very rich and the very poor. She gained my respect immediately as a very savvy woman.

Abdullah did not take the doctor's suggestion seriously. He protested vehemently, saying that the movie was disgusting. He was certain that students didn't act like the ones in the movie. I realized his inability to distinguish fact from fiction.

Dr. Gelt also encouraged Abdullah to see it, thinking it might help him understand Randy and me. Then Dr. Gelt addressed us, "You taught in inner cities, correct?"

We nodded, and I explained that we always established mutual respect so learning could take place. Our first principal, Clarise Stillworth, believed our experiences in the inner city were an asset. She had provided a lot of insight into our unique situation and praised us for our accomplishments.

I thought back to the many students I had while teaching in South Central Los Angeles. Tamika entered my fifth grade class with test scores hovering between the 30th and 40th percentile on her standardized tests. For some reason, she took to me, frequently coming early to school to help organize my classroom and pass out papers. On the playground, we'd sit together and talk about the latest movies we had seen. She and some of her friends used to stand behind me and twist my long straight hair into braids as we watched the boys play ball. I let the girls feel close to me. I wanted them to be comfortable since few white people ever entered their neighborhood. By the end of the year, Tamika's test scores had risen to the 50th percentile. Other parents thanked me for their children's success as well.

By a stroke of good luck, Tamika was in my class again for sixth grade. Her test scores rose again. Since we loved seeing movies, her mom and dad were thrilled when we decided to stay in touch and go see a movie or two together. When she moved on to middle school, her mother called me to let me know that Tamika was becoming increasingly successful. She won a speech contest and graduated with honors from middle school. Tamika's mom thanked me and expressed gratitude that I had always made the students read library books and report on them. When Tamika graduated from Washington High School, she again graduated with honors. She had also won a four-year scholarship to the University of California school systems. The last I'd heard from her, she was taking pre-med classes and dating another pre-med student. I was overjoyed with her continued success and grateful I didn't let her low-test scores dictate my expectations of her in the beginning. Her success was a memory I tucked away for rainy days to remind myself of why I had entered the teaching profession.

Annoyed, Abdullah stood abruptly and announced that we were due at the palace to meet with Their Highnesses. The prince and princess were hosting a luncheon to honor the professors, and we were all invited. Abdullah instructed us not to leave until he was ready and left the room. When Dr. Oman followed immediately behind him, I wondered if the two might be setting a common agenda.

Once Abdullah was gone, Dr. Gelt spoke candidly. "Why would

you want a job like this?"

I said, "We haven't had any problems before. I've loved working here and I like the family. They have a remarkable vision for their children, which we support. We know Abdullah's had conflicts with other teachers, but we thought we could reason with him."

Abdullah returned and said it was time to walk to the palace. Randy and I allowed a slight distance to emerge between the others and us. Randy shook his head. "I can't believe Abdullah contradicted me publicly. First a demotion, and now this, giving someone else credit for my work. And challenging our professionalism?"

We walked by a surveillance camera mounted on the brick wall surrounding the palace, so I spoke softly. "Remember when he said not to mention the proposal to the family?"

"So if it didn't work out, they wouldn't be disappointed?"

"Or so he could give the credit to someone else."

We concluded that Abdullah must indeed be envious of our accomplishments. Besides that, we knew the truth behind the Vanderhort hiring fiasco. To bury his mistake, he might need to bury us. Randy looked dejected, and the stress showed on his face. I despaired seeing such an honest man humiliated but knew he wouldn't be anyone's pawn. I prayed for God to intervene on our behalf.

The small group of American instructors reached the palace grounds. Abdullah led our party up the steps, through the stained glass doors and into the waiting room. He showed the professors where to sit while Randy and I took our seats. Majid and Samira joined us and sat on the couch.

When Prince Faisal and Princess Noura entered, everyone stood. We remained standing as the prince and princess made their rounds, shaking hands and welcoming each person. The handsome couple took their separate chairs and nodded for us to be seated.

The prince pulled out a silver cigarette case. I was surprised since so many in the kingdom considered smoking a sign of decadence.

The prince said, "I have tried to quit many times." He casually inserted the cigarette between his lips. "But I have been unsuccessful. Pardon me, while I light up a cigarette. In the meantime, please accept my apologies for my second-hand smoke. The West convinced us smoking cigarettes was a sign of civilization, but now no one in the West is smoking."

Everyone laughed. I could feel the tension ease with his humor.

He exhaled the smoke into the room of polite visitors. "I suppose that by the time I quit smoking, the West will decide that nothing is wrong with it, so I think I'll continue smoking."

A young Filipina servant entered the room with a silver tray of sparkling fruit drinks in crystal stemware. Each goblet contained a different fruit drink. She quietly circled the room.

The prince set his fruit drink down. "Everyone is saying that this has been a strange year for weather in Saudi Arabia. But this rain is normal for Saudi. Every fifty years we have huge downpours just like the ones we've seen this year. The flowers will be beautiful this spring."

The princess said, "Wild irises will bloom in the desert soon. Mr. and Mrs. Decker, we must take you to see them."

Delighted, I replied, "Your Highness, I'd love to see them. They're my favorite flowers. In fact, we just bought a watercolor of wild irises in the desert."

She smiled and said, "They only bloom for about three weeks, and so we have very little time to see them. We should take a picnic lunch and go to the desert for the whole day." I was honored to be able to see such a beautiful part of God's unique creation in the desert. I also felt like Princess Noura was more comfortable than she ever had been before, and I was pleased she could be herself.

The prince smiled and then offered to give his guests a personal tour of the palace. He mentioned that the palace was small in comparison to the modern palaces currently under construction elsewhere, but he liked the more traditional palace. We followed the prince and princess across the hall into two large rooms. A glass wall separated the family room from a huge indoor pool and patio. The turquoise blue water and white mosaic walls dominated the area and emanated an aura of peaceful rest. Skylights that hovered above it enhanced the beauty of the water. Majestic palms were placed around the tiled deck. The furniture in the family room was mahogany, and the plush carpet was hunter green. On top of an entertainment center was a sprawling fern and numerous family photos in a variety of silver frames.

We continued down a long marble corridor toward the men's section of the palace. It was separate from the family section. Since we were the family's only guests that day, we were allowed a rare glimpse into the life of Saudi princes.

Prince Faisal paused in front of an immense octagonal room that was lined with large windows. Below the windows were satin floor cushions arranged entirely along the perimeters. Between the burgundy cushions were black marble tables covered with silver ashtrays and coasters. A burgundy and blue Persian rug was in the center of the room. A seventy-two inch wide screen TV stood at one end.

The prince explained, "This is where we practice democracy. The members of my family meet with local citizens and then come here to discuss important issues. Every prince has a say, and we abide by the majority."

We wound down corridors admiring an array of antiques, statues, paintings, urns, and tapestries from around the world and felt like we could be in a museum. We passed a curious room that was small and austere. Several dark wooden chairs and a small bench stood along the wall. A navy blue rug covered the ceramic tiled floor. A wooden door painted with geometric designs stood in the corner. A verse from the *Qur'an,* or perhaps the *Shahada,* the declaration of faith, was embroidered with gold thread upon black fabric and hung on the back wall.

The prince pointed to the painted doors. "Doors like these were hung on the first palaces we built in an ancient area known as Diryiah. It's very near Riyadh and surrounded with date palms and streams. These beautiful doors are a part of our heritage. This is also the waiting room for the clerics. In this traditional room, they are comfortable."

Always keeping a delicate balance between the royals and the clerics, I thought, realizing that fundamentalists considered the luxury of wealth decadent, as well as a sign of Western modernization.

We proceeded down additional corridors. Outside, we walked down half a dozen stone steps toward a separate building. It was a large recreational room where the men gathered to watch the national soccer team. Every corner of the room sported a wide screen TV. Soft leather chairs and tables were scattered about the room.

We left the sports room and passed a building with large glass panels for walls. The prince explained that the glass room was used primarily as a sitting room for the men, where they could enjoy a view of the estate gardens. The room looked over a rose garden, a white gazebo, a tennis court and a soccer field. Peaceful palms and acacia trees lined the walls that encompassed the gardens and lawns.

The tour came to an end when a servant approached Prince Faisal and said that lunch was ready. We followed the prince through the remaining gardens, back into the palace and into a formal dining area. As I stepped down toward the sunken floor, I gazed around the lovely room. Large bay windows overlooked the lush green gardens. The stark white walls were decorated with original paintings, mostly oils set in gilded antique frames. A shimmering chandelier draped its graceful arms over the dining table. The white linen tablecloth was embroidered with blue violets. The china service was wedge wood blue. A large floral arrangement of white lilies was set in the center of the table and surrounded by blue candles.

The prince carefully seated his guests. He placed my husband to the right of Princess Noura and me to his left. I was honored by his unexpected show of respect. Hopefully his gesture meant he found us to be loyal and trustworthy employees. The visiting professors were also seated next to the prince and princess.

Along the garden windows stood two tables covered in crisp linen and set with an exquisite silver service. The princess directed our attention toward the luncheon tables and told us to help ourselves. As I was helping myself to the lobster appetizers, I could see Abdullah from the corner of my eye taking the prince by his elbow and whispering into his ear. Something about his manner made me suspicious.

Shortly, Randy approached me and asked, "Where are you sitting?"

"Prince Faisal placed me beside himself, across from Dr. James."

"Abdullah wants you to move."

"But the prince seated everyone himself," I protested.

Abdullah approached and said, "If your husband moves, so should you."

Randy glared at Abdullah and said, "I know what you're doing, Abdullah."

Abdullah's face turned red. Flustered, he returned to the table with an empty dish.

Randy figured Abdullah was moving him so he could sit next to the princess and gain importance in front of the professors. Nevertheless, I was focused on the fact that the prince and princess were pleased that a wonderful opportunity for the children to fulfill a dream was in their grasp.

I said, "But I'm delighted to see Princess Noura beaming. This is her dream."

During dinner Princess Noura carried on a lively conversation with her guests and asked once again if she could take English lessons at our school. She admitted that she was afraid because as a child in an all girls' school, she had been hit with a ruler whenever she made a mistake. I smiled and promised her that we'd lock all rulers in a cabinet and throw away the keys. Since her lessons on *Pride and Prejudice* awaited her in my desk, I encouraged her to come. She smiled contentedly.

Though I was annoyed by Abdullah's slights, I knew the prince and princess were pleased with our performance and the school. I dismissed Abdullah's rudeness but soon learned that I had underestimated his calculated maneuvering.

14.

LEAVING KANSAS

AFTER THE PROFESSORS left Riyadh, Randy and I decided that the school could best continue on course if we overlooked the challenges to our professionalism. The prince and princess were still happy, and we expected everything to settle into a routine. However, a week later, a palace servant whom I had never met before came to bring Majid a change of clothes for his soccer game. Unfortunately, she was the bearer of unsettling developments. More than ever, I missed the honest communication that Clarise had provided and wondered who was whispering into the princess' ear in Machiavellian-like manner. The developments also caused me to wonder about my perception of God's purpose and power.

After Majid took his soccer clothes and left the room, the servant beckoned for me to follow her into a deserted room. She glanced both ways then closed the door and faced me. Whispering, she said, "Things are being said you should know about." She paused for a moment. "The princess thinks you're working with Clarise and the terrorists."

Words of protest were caught in my throat. I felt a trance-like state overcome me.

She shook me as if to wake me up. "You know – the one who threatened to blow up a plane if he didn't get a million dollars. Authorities in several countries are investigating everyone. One of the men sighted in Paris was working with Bin Laden."

Finally, I stammered, "It's, it's not true!"

She shook her head and said, "Powerful people are afraid of losing power. And someone must be angry to link you with this, but I have heard you've done a wonderful job. I don't know what more the princess could want. I must go now, but never mention this conversation to anyone." Pulling her veil and *abaya* tighter around her, she slipped stealthily out of the room. I watched her float down the stairs like a phantom. When she reached the bottom she paused, looked back toward me and placed her fingers over her lips signaling absolute silence. I nodded my agreement, knowing she had taken a grave risk by informing me of the princess' suspicions.

After she left, panic consumed me and I was hounded by haunting questions. Why was she relaying the princess' suspicions to me? Did the servant think I could stop the rumors? Was she warning me to pack while I had time? And who would benefit from planting fear in the mind of the princess? Could the school be in danger of closing again?

Frantically, I ran throughout the building searching for Randy. At last I found him at his desk. Catching my breath I whispered that we had to leave and find a place to talk.

Randy scowled. "I've got work to do."

"My news isn't going to make your work any easier."

We heard the sound of the front door close, but we didn't know if it was Majid or the cleric nosing around.

"Is this about Clarise?" Randy asked.

"In part," I said.

He shuffled his papers into a stack and we left. On the drive home I reminded Randy that Abdullah had taken the key to our villa over Ramadan. The last time we had talked with him, I thought he might be quoting our private conversations, and I wondered if our home might be bugged. I suggested that we take the compound shuttle bus to the mall later that afternoon, thinking that we'd find a place away from surveillance equipment. Once we'd talked things over, I hoped we'd be able to devise a way to stop the rumors and clear our names.

When we arrived home, we took care of the dogs and boarded the shuttle bus. The sun was beginning to set and most people were on their way home from work. At the mall, we wandered around the familiar shops searching for a place to sit. Finally we found an isolated bench that looked over the floors below. Randy seemed annoyed by the inconvenience and insisted I explain what this was about.

I took a deep breath. "A servant came over today with some horrible news. Princess Noura thinks we're working with Clarise and the terrorists."

A dazed look came over him and he stared stoically into the distance. "How can she believe that after all the work we've put into this school for her?"

"How can she believe the rumors about Clarise?"

"I wonder if this terrorist link has anything to do with the way we were searched at the border when we returned from Bahrain? That guard was looking for something."

"I never thought of that," I said. "What are we going to do?"

"We are alone here, so God will have to fight for us," he said.

"Of course. And he will; but with Majid and Samira doing so well, how could anyone be upset? Unless . . ."

Randy faced me with a somber expression. "Unless that's the root of the problem. The kids are prospering, the family likes us, and someone can't stand that. Perhaps we're stealing someone else's show. What if Abdullah is behind this?"

"But the prince told him our relationships are just right. It should have settled this."

"Maybe the religion tutor considers us anti-Islamic. And with all the tension between the clerics and the family . . ."

I kept thinking that since the children were prospering, there shouldn't be any concerns. But Randy pointed out that Majid still wasn't doing well at his Saudi school. In a shame and honor based society, our success could accentuate another's shame. He felt like he was still reading Machiavelli and was lost in intrigue.

"What if we lose everything we've worked for?" I asked distraughtly.

Randy took my hand. "I promise I'll do everything possible to prevent that. We need to talk to Prince Faisal and clear the air. Come on. Let's go home. We need to check on the dogs."

As we headed toward the exit, I felt like I was walking in a dream. Everything around me had lost its glittering allure. The exotic and fascinating items in the stores that had intrigued me when we first arrived held no interest whatsoever. Outside, we waited soberly in the cool night air for the bus to take us home.

Early the next morning, our phone rang. Randy paced back and forth during the conversation and cast alarming looks my way. I shivered when he said that Abdullah wanted us to come into his office. Every time he called I got anxious, remembering how Abdullah's conflict with Mike and Jan escalated so quickly. Randy picked up his cup of cold coffee and tapped it nervously. Abdullah was abrupt on the phone, but Randy thought perhaps the meeting could be an opportunity to solve some misunderstandings.

Even though Abdullah didn't always have good relationships with people, the prince and princess had always been pleased with us and appreciated the work we did with the children. Remembering how the prince had given us seats of honor at the luncheon, we were certain that reason would prevail and God would fight for us. The prince had revealed his respect for us by placing us near him and his wife. Before we left the house, we prayed together and asked God for wisdom, protection and guidance.

We didn't talk much in the car on the way into town. When we arrived at Abdullah's office, we parked on the dry dusty street and slowly climbed the stone steps. The weather was heating up since summer was approaching. I pushed a few strands of hair out of my warm, sticky face. We sat in the reception room and waited restlessly for Abdullah. At last he appeared and motioned for us to enter. For a moment, the room was eerie and quiet.

"So, how was your trip to the mall last night?" Abdullah asked abruptly.

Startled, Randy and I glanced at one another.

"Fine," Randy said curtly.

"You took the bus from the compound. Why didn't you drive?"

My stomach tightened. "How did you know we went to the mall?" I asked.

"A friend of mine said he saw this nice American couple walking around."

"Lots of Americans go to the mall. How did he know it was us?" I asked.

Randy leaned forward. "Geez, we go there all of the time. What's the big deal?"

Laughing slyly he said, "I didn't mean to upset you. This friend just happened to mention that he saw a very nice American couple there."

"When we returned from Bahrain, our car was torn apart by the guard at customs. Do you know anything about it?" asked Randy.

Abdullah said, "How would I know? Of all the people why would he pick you?" Creases appeared on Abdullah's forehead and he looked cagily into Randy's eyes. "Do you know anything about anti-Islamic activity?"

"No! Of course not," Randy declared.

Abdullah turned his head and looked sternly at me. I shook my head fervently.

"What about anti-Islamic groups operating in the city?" he persisted.

"We don't know anything about them," I said indignantly.

"Do you know anything about anti-Islamic literature being distributed throughout Riyadh?"

"Why are you asking us?" demanded Randy.

Abdullah said, "Someone is distributing anti-Islamic literature, some kind of Christian brochure."

"I don't know anything about anti-Islamic activities," said Randy.

"Why would we come to Saudi Arabia if we were anti-Islamic? We're certainly not giving the kids anti-Islamic literature either," I said.

Abdullah glared at me and snapped, "I'd know about it if you were!"

I wondered what had overcome him and where he was going with his questioning. Randy muttered something about searching the internet for information about anti-Islamic groups and promised to get back with Abdullah. Classes were about to begin, so we started to excuse ourselves.

Abdullah had one last order. "Stay after school today. The princess wants to meet with you. She has some concerns."

I dropped my purse on the floor. "Concerns?" I had been counting on the princess and her support if Abdullah ever turned on us. Leaning over, I picked up my bag. The palms of my hands were damp with perspiration.

"Sylvia Vanderhort said some terrible things about you two," he said.

Though we had never met Ms. Vanderhort, Abdullah reveled in her negative reports about our alleged attitude and behavior. He concluded Randy was angry because he would no longer be a director.

Randy shook his head. "It's not my resume that's full of holes, and it was your idea to make me head director. The only thing I care about is the college proposal."

Abdullah sighed. "Yes, yes, I heard all about that."

I mentioned that I had previously spoken with Ms. Vanderhort about Randy's proposal over the phone. "When I told Sylvia that Randy wrote the proposal, I wanted to honor my husband."

Abdullah's face darkened, and he peered at me as if I were a child. "What is this talk about honoring your husband? It was the prince's idea!"

Randy rolled his eyes. "Abdullah, what are you going to do about this woman's poor recommendation from her last supervisor? She was a troublemaker."

Abdullah was silent, so Randy said, "I can document that with names and phone numbers."

At the mention of direct evidence, Abdullah became extremely tense and nervously tapped a pencil on the desk. He must have been worried that Randy had checked the references and he hadn't. What lengths would his shame cause him to go to hide his inefficiency?

"Stay after school today," Abdullah repeated.

"We should meet with Prince Faisal and clear the air," said Randy.

Abdullah's eyes flashed with rage. He bolted out of his chair and yelled at Randy, "He doesn't want to talk with you!"

I was terrified by his outrage. My hands were shaking and I wanted to leave immediately. The prince had always been open to talking with us in the past, and I was bewildered. Fortunately, Randy remained steady and persistent, asking to meet with Prince Faisal in order to answer any concerns about our character and conduct.

Abdullah pounded the desk with his fist. "You will meet with the princess. Be at the school this evening!" Abdullah turned away and stared out his office window toward a small garden with stunted palms.

"Fine," stammered Randy.

Randy flung the office door wide open; it rattled against the wall. I hurried out of the room behind him. The only sound in the building was the quick clicking of our shoes on the marble floors as we headed directly for the exit. I was shaking from the intense confrontation, and I couldn't wait to get out of the building.

Once outside, Randy opened the car door for me and fumed, "What is he up to?"

"Did he have someone follow us?" I asked. "And why? We have always supported the princess. This doesn't make any sense at all."

Randy started the car and pulled out onto the dusty street. "It doesn't look like Abdullah can listen to reason. God will help us clear our good names. It's easy to trust him when everything is going smoothly. Now we'll have to trust him through the dark time."

"I never thought Abdullah would be so unreasonable with us. I trusted him," I said.

"Look, he didn't like Clarise and he didn't like the principal before her. He didn't like Mike and Jan. He took away my contributions and made me look bad for claiming them. It's a pattern."

"Jan's neighbor, that cowboy, tried to tell me, but I didn't listen to him. I thought we were different."

Randy and I agreed that if Abdullah had a hidden agenda, he'd do whatever it took to implement it. What we said wouldn't matter one iota. We wondered if he wanted us out of Saudi, but since the kids had responded so well to us, he couldn't be the one pointing the finger. If we didn't get through to the prince, Abdullah could ruin another school.

We continued our ride in silence. When I entered the school foyer, I entered with a heavy, grieving heart. If God would just grant me the right words when we spoke with the princess, perhaps our collective dreams could continue. While preparing for class, I kept thinking about what had happened to Clarise and the Barkers. When the bell rang, I was still trembling and could feel tears welling up in my eyes. Why didn't my prayers calm my frazzled nerves?

Samira entered the room quietly. "Mrs. Decker, are you alright?"

I wasn't sure how much I should say but decided upon candor. "I'm upset about Abdullah."

She looked at me sympathetically. "He's not nice to people. I tried to tell you."

"Yes, you did, but I thought the Barkers might be most of the problem. Now Abdullah's questioning us about anti-Islamic activity."

"Abdullah is not worth your tears, Mrs. Decker. He can't hold a candle to you. You have so much more integrity than he does. He's lower than a rat! And when I have a school for my own children, I'm going to be directly involved, so I know what's going on." She reached for her book and opened it up but simply stared at the pages.

This beautiful young woman never ceased to amaze me with her wisdom and bold insight. I was grateful she considered me a person of integrity because she was special to me, and I respected her opinion. Gazing at the poster of the goals she'd made the first day of school, I prayed for her future. She had a caring heart and the potential to make noteworthy contributions to her world.

When the bell rang, Samira stood slowly. She walked around the desk and put her arms around me. "I'm sorry; I'm not very good at this."

As she embraced me, I said, "This hugging is an American thing." I smiled at her, and she walked sadly out of the room. We both knew that men would be the ones taking care of business.

For the next half hour, I stared mindlessly out the window and watched the limbs of the acacia tree quiver in the wind and beat against the window pain. How was I going to stop the cascading chain of events? And when would God intervene?

Later in the afternoon when the Arab tutors arrived, I was working on the computer next to Majid. One of the male tutors stood directly behind Majid, observing his work. Unfortunately, the cleric was sneaking around the school. When he walked past the computer room, he cast a fiercely scolding frown my way. Since mixed company was forbidden, the tutor froze and the cleric bristled. Suddenly, the cleric vanished. I was afraid what he might do or say next.

Later, when everyone had left the school, I walked upstairs to a quiet room where I could be alone and knelt to pray.

"Dear Lord," I began fervently, "You have led us here and caused our hands to prosper. Now we need your wisdom. Fill us with an abundance of your Spirit." For the next half hour I beseeched the Lord, asking for his strength. I asked for the right words so we could reach an understanding with the princess. God's presence flooded the room.

Whatever happened, I knew he was with me.

Soon George knocked on the door. He had come to assist with the meeting and had already spoken with the princess and Abdullah downstairs. On our way down, Randy quietly joined us from a classroom. George took him by the arm and told him to be strong. Randy and I nodded. We were anxious to set the record straight. I was unaware though, of how embedded and controlling one's defense mechanisms could be. Nor did I understand the sense of intrigue and tribalism that defined convenient alliances stronger than truth and justice.

In the teachers' workroom, we pulled the chairs out and sat around the table. The sun had set and we couldn't see the garden. I could only hear the wind rush through the palms as Princess Noura strode sternly into the room and sat at the head of the table. I had never seen this side of her. Her lips were tightly pursed; her eyes were cold. Abdullah followed closely behind her, his head raised haughtily into the air like a schoolboy who'd won a fight on the playground.

The princess immediately addressed Randy. "Would you like to start speaking, or should I?" She was silent for a moment. After glancing at Abdullah, she spoke. "I will begin. There are some things going on that I do not like. First, have I ever come into your house to judge your religion?"

"No," said Randy.

"Then why do you come into my house and judge my religion? This is unacceptable. You are not to speak about your religion!" she snapped.

"We only talk about the things Islam and Christianity have in common," I said, wondering what she had been told. Besides, when the children talked about Islam, I was glad to learn more about it.

She failed to acknowledge me and studied a piece of paper in her hands. She continued, "Haven't I provided you with a house and a car? And haven't you been paid on time? And didn't I let you go to Bahrain? Is there any part of the contract I have not kept?"

"You have kept the contract," said Randy. "Everything you've mentioned has been in order."

The princess said, "And the university professors. You yelled at them! You insulted me by discussing personal business about my husband and myself. You told them to ask if my husband and I have different goals for the school."

Randy glanced at Abdullah and then at the princess. "Not exactly."

The princess said, "This is none of your business. I hired you to teach. These people were my guests. It is my right to have them."

Randy nodded. "Of course it is, Your Highness. It was my idea to create a relationship . . ."

" . . . And furthermore, Mr. Decker," she interrupted, "you keep insisting it was your idea to invite the professors. It was not your idea. It was my husband's!"

"Well, maybe we both thought of it at . . ."

"This school is my dream!" She slammed her fist into the table and leaned forward, her eyes filled with tears and anger. "You, Mr. Decker, have completely ruined it!"

Silence consumed the room and ate at us like a cancer. Randy and I were shocked by the distortions. I agonized for my husband because he had done so much for the school. Suddenly the beleaguered princess glanced at her diamond-studded watch. Abdullah encouraged her to go ahead and leave, promising to take care of business for her.

She stood abruptly, gathering her *abaya* and purse. She was on her way to a party with relatives.

I gasped as she rose.

She looked sternly down her nose toward me. "What?" she demanded.

"Don't we get to talk to you?" I asked distraughtly.

She tossed her head high. "Tell Abdullah everything!"

My heart sank. Her decision to leave the room would leave her in utter darkness about her very own children. In that moment, she lost her dreams, my husband was dishonored, and I was crushed by my inability to reason through the crisis. But I also realized that the decision to leave and not listen was her decision, not mine.

Princess Noura strode arrogantly toward the door, ordering Abdullah to have video cameras installed in every classroom. After apologies all around, she and Faisal would decide what to do. She marched down the corridor, leaving us in the hands of an angry man who had come to despise us.

Randy and I turned our attention toward Abdullah. Randy told him we had a letter for him.

He held up his hand. "No letters from you."

I thought of the words of forgiveness we wanted to extend and encouraged him to read it. He grabbed the folded letter from my hands and opened it. After a moment he blurted, "This makes me look like the bad guy!" He wadded it up and threw it savagely to the ground, our offer of forgiveness scorned.

"But, Abdullah, you are making these charges up," I said. "We're the ones feeling insulted."

Abdullah launched into an animated and defensive tirade. "What have I ever done to you? You have been paid. We let you go to

Bahrain. Your villa is nice. Have I ever failed to pay you?"

While these may have been issues with previous employees, payment wasn't our issue. Repeating them made Abdullah appear like a broken record reciting old conversations.

He ranted on. "And you insulted me when you walked down the stairs at the school. The person coming down the stairs is supposed to say 'hello' first."

"When was that?" asked Randy. "I don't know that custom, and you've been the one who's always explained such customs to us."

Suddenly, Abdullah looked ashamed for he had indeed been the mediator who proudly explained Arab customs. Nevertheless, he proceeded with his accusations. "You've been manipulative. You have been putting on a big act. What have I done to you?"

I said, "Well, look at you now. You're calling us manipulative. You're saying we are acting. You're not listening to us."

He stopped the personal accusations. "People only come here because they are greedy."

I peered directly into his eyes and challenged him. "Are you saying we are greedy?"

"No!" Abdullah looked away.

I tried to reason with him. "Let's put this behind us for the good of the children."

He ignored me. "Your Highness wants letters of apology. You should apologize for insulting Their Highnesses, me and Sylvia Vanderhort."

Sylvia Vanderhort? I was appalled but Randy diplomatically agreed to write the letters.

I searched for the right words that would pierce the veil that kept Abdullah a captive of darkness. "The children shouldn't suffer because adults cannot forgive one another."

Abdullah would not look me in the eye. "You are manipulative and insubordinate."

"Abdullah, please, let's put this behind us," I pleaded.

He spit the words out again. "You are manipulative."

"Let's put this behind us," I repeated.

But Abdullah sat paralyzed in the grips of vindictiveness, unable to turn the key of forgiveness that would unlock him from its rancid prison. "My family has been here for three generations. My grandfather served the royal family, as did my father. So who do you think you are, Mr. Randy Decker?"

That was it. His last question revealed all Abdullah cared about, position. He didn't care about the children, and he resented our rapport and success with them.

Randy stared at him in shock and then whispered to me, "We do not deserve to be spoken to like this, especially not after all we've done for the family. I'll contact the prince directly."

The princess had walked out and Abdullah was unable to listen. I agreed with my husband. I looked sadly at George who had remained silent during the proceedings. I told him though I wanted to stay for the children, I would not be spoken to so cruelly.

Randy and I stood together. I leaned over Abdullah and placed my hand squarely on his shoulder. "God will forgive you for this, and so do we."

He shuddered with utmost disdain, wriggling his shoulder out from underneath my firm grasp. Whether he shuddered because I was simply an infidel or a woman, I didn't care.

George nodded with understanding. Randy and I walked down the corridor as Abdullah yelled after us with an order to turn in our resignation the next day. We said a heartfelt good-bye to dear Seddar, the gatekeeper. He was sad and fearful as he shook our hands. I assumed he would be punished if he showed us any sympathy.

Randy drove quickly along the dark city streets toward home. As we approached our compound, I gazed mournfully over the rugged horizon in the distance. Suddenly, a brilliant falling star streaked through the ebony sky. Never before had I seen such a vibrant and dazzling burst of light and hoped that it was some kind of divine, good omen, some sign of God's providence and approval. I took some comfort in the affirmation from the heavens.

An hour later, George and Lydia arrived at our villa. Lydia couldn't believe we didn't get a hearing even if we had made a mistake here or there. George added, "Neither of you are allowed to return to the school. Abdullah told Seddar not to let you enter. I have to pack up your teaching materials."

"And the children have been forbidden to speak your names," Lydia said hesitantly.

I felt like a knife had been stabbed into my heart and turned mercilessly. We hadn't even said good-bye to them or to the others we cared about.

George said, "When I met with Abdullah, he listed some negative behaviors he wanted me to watch for in you."

Randy said, "I'm not surprised. He had us watch Clarise's spending at the school. And he tried to get me to move into her office and take over her job. I suspect he's been trying to have this Vanderhort woman do the same to us. If she were smarter, she'd have seen through it."

When I asked Lydia what traits they were supposed to watch for, she said territorialism and insubordination. I was puzzled for all of our relationships had emerged naturally, and we were committed to the family's dream. "What does he mean by that?"

George said, "Don't take it to heart. We've never seen anything like that in your behavior. We know how hard you've worked, and we know how positive you've been about Saudi Arabia."

Lydia added, "You have our complete support. Our prayer group is praying for you."

"I'll still write the apologies and try to resolve this diplomatically," said Randy.

George promised to check on us in the morning. Lydia encouraged me to call her even if it was in the middle of the night. Our dear friends who had championed our success left our home filled with sadness and disbelief.

Randy said he was beginning to feel like Mordecai, a man whose life was described in the Old Testament book of Esther. Mordecai, a Jewish man living in exile under the Persian king Ahasuerus, had discovered a plot to overthrow the king. When Mordecai explained the plot to Queen Esther, who also was his uncle's daughter, the vile plot was intercepted and the perpetrators captured. Mordecai's deed went unrecognized. Later, a Persian courtier, Haman, was angry with Mordecai for not bowing before him and revering him in the manner in which his position commanded. Haman plotted Mordecai's death as well as the death of all Jews living in Persia. He accused the Jews of failing to honor the king and obtained permission to destroy them. Fortunately, Queen Esther wisely intervened with the king on Mordecai's behalf. His life, as well as the lives of all Jews in the Persian kingdom, was spared. Mordecai's good deeds came to light and he was publicly honored for saving the king's life. Haman hung on the gallows he had prepared for Mordecai.

Randy and I needed someone to intervene on our behalf like Esther had for Mordecai. In the past, Clarise had kept the paths of communication clear. Sadly, Clarise had been surreptitiously removed from power, and Abdullah abhorred our attempts to communicate with the family. He had given away the credit for Randy's contributions to another. Nevertheless, Randy was hopeful that if he could meet with the prince himself, he'd be able to prevent the defamation of our character and protect our jobs. I knew that my husband had a good chance to do so, knowing how analytical and articulate he was. We also decided that we'd go to the American embassy on the following morning and try to work through diplomatic channels.

15.

"DHIMMI"

THE PRINCESS HAD requested letters of apology, so Randy stayed up until after midnight at the computer, writing and rewriting them. I came downstairs several times encouraging him to go to bed. When he finally came upstairs, we stayed up most of the night talking anxiously, trying vainly to understand how everything became so twisted and asking God to help us. I wondered what would transpire next and if reason would prevail or if God would deliver us. Would I tread a path along the valley of the shadow of death as Mike and Jan had? And how would I respond to this ever-darkening cloud of evil?

We downed our morning coffee, hoping it would help us stay alert. Soon we drove to the diplomatic quarters to pursue a proper resolution. The entrance to the international embassies was cordoned off at a circle drive by a roadblock. Armed Saudi guards carefully checked cars and drivers. Once cleared, we drove toward the American embassy. Randy parked on the street and we headed for the next security check. Though a peaceful waterfall flowed freely down a marble wall in front of the U.S. embassy, the building was completely surrounded with high iron fences and thick cement blocks covered with potted plants. Once through the barriers, a Marine searched us at a booth where all of our bags were thoroughly inspected. Our bags were searched again, and then we finally walked through a metal detector.

We found the registration office and waited impatiently in line. When we reached the front, we spoke with two male clerks and explained our circumstances. One clerk shrugged his shoulders and wanted to know who was handling it. When we said Abdullah Al-Rasheed, the two men looked at one another.

Randy asked, "Do you know this man?"

"We know him. He used to work here."

Randy said, "We want to speak with the prince, but Abdullah won't schedule a meeting."

The first clerk hesitated. "We know this prince and have a good relationship with him."

Randy frowned. "What does that mean?"

"Do you have plane tickets home?" the second clerk asked.

"We'll get them this afternoon," I replied. "But we don't want to go home."

"Take the tickets and go home," he advised.

Randy tapped his fingers nervously on the shelf. I pleaded with the clerks. "But we don't even know what we did."

One let out an exasperated sigh. "You must have done something to make them so mad."

Frustrated I said, "We only want an audience with the prince."

"Well, be careful. You don't want to end up in a Saudi jail," warned the other. "Especially when the guards find out who you work for. They're very loyal to this prince."

"Thanks for the help," Randy quipped. He spun around and headed for the exit. Speaking loud enough for everyone to hear, he said, "These people don't care about justice."

As we left the office I recalled the words of Edmond Burk, quoted by Martin Luther King in a letter he wrote while imprisoned in the Birmingham jail, *Injustice anywhere is a threat to justice everywhere.* I hoped those in authority would take words like these to heart but feared Randy and I were mere expenditures in the pursuit of an illusive political policy of appeasement. Were we idealists to believe in justice? I was beginning to think that a spirit of Machiavellian nature had manifested and was thwarting all of our efforts to pursue justice. Certainly, a battle of some sorts, perhaps a spiritual battle, was occurring.

We walked forlornly outside and sat on a marble wall in front of the waterfall. We listened to the water trickle over small rocks as it hit the bottom. A few birds landed on the plaza in front of us. The lonely American flag flapped in the desert breeze. Though my surroundings provided an aura of peace, my inner world was unraveling. I now understood why Mike and Jan had considered U.S. embassies worthless. If diplomacy wasn't going to work, we were at a loss as to what to do next. It was appearing more and more like I wouldn't be able to avoid walking through a valley of the shadow of death where our dreams would be lost.

We left the embassy and when we arrived home, Akbar was waiting with more bad news. He bowed his head sadly and told us he needed to return our car to the palace and then drive us to a lawyer. Randy looked frustrated because we needed the car to take the dogs to the vet for their traveling papers.

Akbar lowered his eyes. Randy placed his hand on his shoulder and said, "It's not your fault."

"Thank you, sir. You always good to me."

Reluctantly, Randy handed the keys over to Akbar. We got in the back, so he could drive us into the city for a business meeting. We arrived at an unfamiliar, austere brick building and walked up a dim flight of steps and entered a strange office. A gray haired man of Middle Eastern descent introduced himself as the family's attorney and motioned for us to take a seat. Though I trusted Akbar, I had no idea who this man was or what he might do, or if an attorney would be provided to represent us.

Nonchalantly, the attorney pulled out a large manila file. "Well, these things happen," he said.

Irritated by his lack of concern, I snapped, "They shouldn't."

He dropped the file on his desk. "Let's sign the documents, so you can get your passports, pay and plane tickets back to the United States. Out of the goodness of their hearts, Their Highnesses will give you two weeks pay."

I was stunned. "Two weeks! Our contract guaranteed three months." A list of our expenditures flashed through my mind, and I panicked, wondering how we would keep current with our bills and mortgage in America.

The lawyer scowled. "They don't have to give you anything under the circumstances."

Randy's face turned red. "Under the circumstances? The contract we signed in the States didn't list circumstances. It said everything would be settled amicably. And furthermore, we haven't even had an audience with the prince."

The lawyer stared down his nose. "The charges are very serious."

I glared at him. "We don't even know what the charges are!"

The lawyer abruptly excused himself and walked out the door. Randy opened his appointment book and scribbled something. The lawyer returned with a palace servant who would be an eyewitness. After a quick nod of acknowledgement, the servant sat down. The lawyer handed our passports and paychecks to the man and proceeded.

"The matter is settled. You will get two weeks pay. Sign on the ledger you have received it."

"What are we being charged with?" I asked. The lawyer ignored me.

Randy grabbed the ledger and read it carefully. The amount of pay wasn't accurate. Randy explained that the amount was based on the wrong pay scale because our annual payments had been stretched from ten to twelve months. As a result, our monthly paychecks were much lower.

The lawyer squirmed in his stuffed leather chair. "You have a home in America, don't you?"

I could feel my breathing quicken. "It's rented."

"Have the renters move out. You'll be fine," he said curtly.

My heart raced. "We won't break a lease. What kind of people do you think we are?"

I tried to control my rapid breathing. I finally decided to sign the ledger and said, "But for the record, I want it known that I am signing it under protest because the amount is wrong and the charges made up." The futility of seeking reconciliation finally sank in. I burst into sobs and started shaking uncontrollably. "Oh, Lord," I cried, "We'll lose everything we've worked for!"

Randy said, "Sweetheart, sweetheart!"

The lawyer shouted, "Oh, no, Mrs. Decker, we can't have this! No duress! No duress!"

Was that an order or a statement, I wondered. Looking through my disheveled bangs and tears, I said, "Oh, give me the damned papers. I'll sign them. Just get me out of here!" Randy put his arm around me, but I couldn't control my sobbing. I waved a pen in the air and searched frantically for the documents. "I'll sign it. Just get me out of here!"

The lawyer bolted around his desk, mumbling to himself about duress. He grabbed the documents and darted from the room.

Randy held my hand. "Try to hold on, sweetheart. I'm taking notes in case we can sue them." But I wondered if the room might be equipped with surveillance monitors.

From the corner of my eye, I could see our passports in the witness's trembling hand. When the lawyer returned, he motioned for the witness to follow him out the door. Our passports were tossed casually on the desk. Why hadn't we insisted on keeping our passports in our possession?

A few moments later, the lawyer returned alone. He had called George and Lydia Phelps to be eyewitnesses. He suggested that we would be more comfortable with them, but I laughed at the explanation.

The lack of concern from people I cared about was excruciating. I kept wondering why no one would listen to us, why we didn't have any legal representation, and how the prince and princess could turn on us so quickly. Was it more important for them to be right rather than caring? And what good were religious rules if the end result prevented caring? Were we being vilified so injustice could be sanctioned? I begged God for his mercy and deliverance.

"I want out of this office and I want out of this stupid country!" I fumed. While I regretted saying the country was stupid, nothing was making any logical sense. I hated that room. If justice was going to be denied to us, I simply wanted my passport, paycheck and a safe place to cry.

The attorney said, "The Phelps will be here soon. In the meantime, I have some documents for you to sign saying you will not pursue a lawsuit." The lawyer left again.

I threw my hands into the air. "Good grief! They're asking us to sign our rights away. We must be under surveillance. They probably saw you taking notes or heard you talking."

"Look, honey, right now they're changing the witness to someone who didn't see you cry. If you can hold on, we'll get out of here sooner, and I can pursue other courses. God will help us find a way through this somehow."

We could hear the attorney talking with someone in the hallway. When he returned, he put a paper in front of us that stated we wouldn't sue anyone involved with our deportation. We started to sign it, but the lawyer grabbed it out of our hands and left again. Soon, the lawyer returned with another paper. Additional names had been added to the list. We signed the document; the lawyer gathered the papers and headed for the door.

I was emotionally and physically drained. We had no rights, no power and no voice. After what seemed like hours, George and Lydia appeared at the door. Their faces were sullen and downcast. George said that they came as quickly as they could.

The lawyer forced a wooden smile. "Now, Mr. and Mrs. Decker, you will be comfortable. You can get your pay and passports and be on your way home to America."

I tried desperately to maintain my composure so I could leave that prison of a room. The lawyer set our passports and paychecks on the table. We signed the papers and rose to leave. Randy grabbed the passports and checks, and I picked up the plane tickets and letters of dismissal. At the doorway, I opened my letter to find out what the charges were. I was being accused of insulting Their Highnesses, insulting Islam and exhibiting a pattern of insubordination. I felt utterly betrayed. Devastated, I hung my head. My signature was on the bottom line.

Randy pushed me forward, saying he would still try to talk to the prince. He led me hastily by the hand downstairs and outside. We approached the car where Akbar was waiting. Within minutes, George and Lydia joined us. Lydia's eyes were moist and empathic.

"This whole thing is a sham," I exclaimed. "I signed the papers just to get out of there. I can't believe people do business like this. Even Mike and Jan didn't go through this, and Mike was openly angry with Abdullah. At least we've been trying to resolve it diplomatically."

I asked Lydia with whom the lawyer was talking in the hall.

She breathed deeply before saying, "Abdullah Al-Rasheed."

Randy went into a slump as if he'd been hit in the stomach, and my heart sank. Abdullah must have been behind everything, and we should have realized we would fare no better than those who came before us. Our pride prevented us from seeing that we were neither any better off nor any wiser.

"He ruined our school, and now he's ruined yours," said George.

"Why would the prince and princess listen to him?" I asked.

"The word of a Muslim is always believed before the word of a non-Muslim, and a man's word before a woman's," explained Lydia. "Even if that word is obviously false. I've seen the students follow that closely when deciding an issue."

"Guess that makes two sides of a story completely meaningless," said Randy. "It's sure a different concept of justice."

"Loyalty and tribalism have their own kind of truth," George said. He turned to Akbar and told him that Abdullah wanted him to drive to our compound with some workers from the palace and pack up our belongings. Sadly, Akbar agreed. Randy was relieved it was Akbar rather than a cold-hearted stranger.

Randy fumbled through the papers and saw that our departure time was 3:00 a.m. that very morning. "Geez, that doesn't leave time to appeal this."

"That's the point," said George.

He reminded us that in the old days, *dhimmi*, the Christians and Jews who were considered people of the book, had second-class status in Islamic society and weren't allowed to access the justice system. * Though they were allowed to practice their own religion, they were required to pay special taxes and were subordinate to Muslims. In court, their words were meaningless. Indeed, the *Caliph* of Baghdad forced Jews to wear a yellow badge for identification, a practice later revived under the Nazi regime. *

George continued, "That kind of thinking can still surface. Besides, if you go through the Saudi justice system, you'd end up telling your story to the Governor of Riyadh. Then he would learn Faisal and Noura defied him by opening their school against his wishes. He'd be furious, and who knows what he would do? Prince Faisal would be greatly shamed."

"But if we don't speak up for ourselves, our lives here are ruined," I said.

"We're between the rock and the hard place once again," sighed Randy. "And this time we might be crushed."

"Whatever happens, nothing is worth compromising your integrity," said George.

Randy said, "This will not destroy our character. It will reveal it."

Abdullah had sunk to the level of lying and subterfuge to achieve his purposes and maintain his status. Perhaps he had saved face, but at what cost to his soul, the children and all of those around him?

George and Lydia drove us back to the compound and left us at our villa, promising to return later. When I saw my dogs, I put my arms around their necks and thanked the Lord for their selfless devotion and loving comfort. Cheyenne licked my face and Aslan pawed at me innocently. I studied their dark brown eyes and saw tender love. They needed to be walked, so I put the leashes carefully around their necks. As I walked around the compound and gazed at the familiar surroundings that had become home, I interceded with God to work on our behalf and give us a voice.

When I returned, Randy and I went to talk with Seid and say our good-byes. When we found him at the recreation center, Seid explained that the same kind of injustice happens to his people constantly. Apparently, the Indian embassy could do nothing. It had no influence or leverage with the Saudi government. The Saudi government considered India as a source of cheap, expendable labor and looked the other way at rumors of slave labor.

Randy asked, "If things are so bad, why don't people just go back to India?"

"Saudi sponsors keep passports. And my people are afraid of Saudis; afraid of torture or rape. So they camp at our embassies. No one listens to us."

"Why not?" I asked.

"Saudis call us *dhimmi*, people of second-class, of *Dar Al-Harb*. We do not have the same rights. We are not equal. Our word no good in court."

Lydia and George had previously explained the difference between *Dar Es-Salam* and *Dar Al-Harb*. The two competing states were in a constant strife with one another. *

"But even though they paid a special tax, the prophet, Mohammed, allowed Jewish and Christian communities to live among Muslims. That's where the word *dhimmi* comes from," I protested.

"Yes, I have heard this," agreed Seid. "But his words are forgotten or twisted. You are Americans. Americans will care. People will listen to you. Please, fight for me and my people!"

I was honored by Seid's belief in America's sense of justice, but I didn't know what we could do. Perhaps Seid was showing me a way to care for others and heal my own wounds. Perhaps in my losses, shedding light on the welfare of others would help me channel our unfortunate circumstances toward benefiting others.

"Ma'am, God will show you what to do. And, Ma'am, I saw you have a Bible. I wonder if I could use it. I am Christian. In India, the missionaries taught me."

"You can have it if you leave it for the next Christian who comes here. Maybe it will give strength to others who need it."

"Ma'am," said Seid, "I am honored. I have no Bible for many years."

"His Word is a light in the darkness, and it's the power to salvation. May it bless many who come here."

Randy smiled and reached for my hand. "We'd better head back toward the villa. The palace workers will arrive any minute to pack our things, and I want to make some more phone calls so we don't find ourselves heading out of Saudi Arabia on the next flight."

I sought refuge by meditating upon the verses of Psalm Twenty-three, where the psalmist David wrote, *Yea, though I walk through the valley of the shadow of death, I will fear no evil, for Thou art with me. Thy rod and Thy staff, they comfort me.* Suddenly, I had new insight into the passage. Though evil existed in the world, and I would be exposed to it, I would not need to fear it. Evil could not overcome me to the point I would violate my integrity for an inauspicious goal. The strength to maintain integrity came directly from the Lord. I thanked God for His empowering wisdom and grace in a time of need. He was with me, guiding the ethical decisions of my heart and releasing me from the vileness of hatred and the stench of revenge. He was leading me toward loving kindness and forgiveness. I prayed for mercy to follow in my path and rule my heart.

Though my faith had been renewed and strengthened, reason and diplomacy had failed. Randy and I returned to our villa, hoping for a miracle that would change the unfolding course of events. If God didn't intervene on our behalf, we'd have no other alternative but to board the plane bound for America and leave our dreams and hearts behind in Saudi Arabia.

16.

FREE

EVERY ATTEMPT TO communicate with Prince Faisal was thwarted by Abdullah, and every word we spoke misrepresented. We despaired the fact that Prince Faisal believed we had cursed his family, but the separation was final and complete. We were considered despised outcasts who had earned the fate of ill treatment. During our last few hours, our Muslim and Christian friends gathered around to console us. Though from a simple life, I hungered for their affection, respect and words of comfort. In them, I saw character, morality and a reason to tell our combined stories.

Randy and I clutched our paychecks, passports and plane tickets. George, Lydia, Akbar and Mohammed Habib drove us to the airport. Heartbroken, Randy and I said our good-byes and boarded the plane headed toward America. It was 3:00 a.m. I tossed and turned in the small seat, searching for peace of mind. Since sleep eluded me, I turned toward Randy, seeking reassurance that we were doing the right thing by getting off the plane when it landed in Athens.

"I think it's the best we can do, especially in light of the threats Abdullah made. He was so unreasonable bullying his way through conflicts like that. And I'm worried about what he could do next."

I shuddered and said, "hen I think of the way Clarise and Hunter were treated and that they weren't allowed to return to Saudi Arabia. And I desperately need some sleep."

"Me too," said Randy. "At least Clarise is safe in America and far away from the long arms of Saudi justice."

My thoughts returned to the villa in Saudi we had been forced out of just hours earlier. I asked Randy what Akbar had said to him on the porch before he took the dogs to the vet.

Randy rested his head against the seat. "Well, his eyes clouded up and then he said I was a good man."

In some ways, I felt like I was seeing Randy for the very first time. "You always had the best of intents, and it upsets me to think of how Abdullah treated you after your devotion to the family."

"Thank you, sweetheart. It's Akbar I'll never forget. He was such a good person. And he did so much for us, especially when we needed him. If it hadn't been for Akbar, Aslan and Cheyenne would've been left behind to wander the desert."

"Abdullah only cared about saving face, but everyone knew what he was like."

"I'd never have imagined he was so duplicitous when we met him at the job fair," I said. "But a quiver ran down my spine when I first saw him. I just ignored it when we actually met him."

Thinking about the words of Immanuel Kant, *You can tell the heart of a man by his treatment of animals*, provided some insight into Abdullah. I concluded that his heart must have been hardened, frightened and insecure.

Randy added, "Abdullah presented himself as intelligent and modern, but it cost a lot to trust him."

We would need to cash out most of our meager teachers' retirement to keep the house, and it would take years to recover financially. Our resumes were a mess now, and our credit would be ruined. I looked away.

"Look, things happen for a reason. I would do this again."

I searched his eyes hoping to find forgiveness. "Even knowing everything you do now?"

"Yes, we'll find meaning in this." He paused. "Last night I had a dream. I dreamed that a huge dark cloud hovered all over Sauid Arabia. The cloud kept descending, getting darker and more oppressive. I started to pray that God would come and burst through the cloud and break it up with a bolt of lightning. But then, I looked out over the desert and saw pools of blood scattered across the sands as far as I could see. All at once, the blood turned into beams of light and pushed the cloud back. I could feel the cloud get weaker, and then suddenly the light from the pools covered the whole land. That was when I understood. It's the blood of Christ and the suffering of his people that will break the power of darkness."

Randy's dream brought to mind an experience I'd had before we left America. "Let me tell you what happened while taking the Eucharist one Sunday. I was meditating upon Christ on the cross and my forgiveness when I felt like he asked me if I would die for him. I interpreted it symbolically, like a death to self or a dream, and said, 'Yes.'"

"Maybe, then, this unexpected turn of events really isn't outside of God's will for us. Akbar was surprised by our response. He expected me to take revenge and offered to take it on my behalf. Even George and Mohammed wondered why we weren't boiling over with anger and rage."

"Then perhaps the best deliverance is to be free from revenge," I sighed. "God did strengthen us. In a way, this has lifted a veil from my own understanding. What is most important are the things I've taken for granted, like our marriage and our home. Still, it's going to take a long time to recover emotionally. And the children . . ."

"I know." Randy stared past me and out the dark window. "That's the hardest part for me. Abdullah didn't affect me because everything he said was such nonsense. But losing sight of a dream and the connection with the children." Randy was silent. "That's what hurts."

I could sense the heavy beating of his heart when I added, "I guess that's the risk we took when we let ourselves care about them. But that's who we are, and I wouldn't change it. I hope Majid and Samira grow up and do the good things they wanted to." I hoped that if they learned from the experiences of Prince Jen and Prince Hamlet, it would make our losses more bearable. I would always pray that they have a heart for the less fortunate among them.

Randy said, "Maybe we didn't come here to just help a prince, but to care for people like Akbar and Seid."

"Who'd want to be rich and powerful if you couldn't treat people right?" I said.

Randy said, "You know, when we get off the plane in Athens, no one will know where we are. We'll feel safe and have time to sort things out."

Sort things out. His words echoed throughout my mind. There were other things I needed to tell him, feelings deep within that were now swimming to the surface and denying me rest. Our losses in Saudi Arabia must have triggered familiar emotions. I stared out the side window into the vast night sky, hoping to find the right words. "And, and . . . there's something I want to tell you." I turned toward him but cast my eyes downward and stared at my wedding ring.

Randy took my hands, held them and rubbed his finger over my beautiful ring. "What sweetheart?"

"I could never have made it through this without you. I've always thought I was the strong one in our relationship, but I was wrong. You are, and I . . . I really need you now." Tears swelled in my eyes, but this time they were tears of deep relief and healing.

He lifted my face by the chin and met my eyes. "I know you love me, but I've felt I couldn't live up to your expectations."

Though astonished, I was glad he could be honest with me. "I've made you feel like you weren't good enough for me? How?"

"Well, like when you kept pushing me to be the director of the school. I felt like being a regular teacher wasn't good enough, and . . ."

" . . . I am so sorry. I had no idea." I buried my face in his warm shoulder and whispered, "I don't know why it's so hard for me to tell you how much you mean to me."

"I know you well enough by now to understand," he paused. "You've always had to go it alone to follow your dreams, but you're not alone anymore. You have me; it was your father who refused to help and support you. I know you felt invisible around him, and sometimes, I think he colors your view of life altogether."

Grasping Randy's hand, I finally allowed the terrifying and ghostly images of violence and repeated beatings to float into my consciousness. I recalled the screaming, hollering and beatings in my childhood home, the anger, the constant conflict and hatred. I felt the bruises of those around me and recalled the consequent excuses from my father. I remembered the fist poised to pummel my face. The sense of worthlessness and shame overwhelmed me, but now my feelings defied me and poured into my consciousness like waves pounding the sands. I broke into sobs.

"You're right," I admitted. "He said he wanted me to fail, so I'd lose my faith in Christ." I hesitated before saying, "But it wasn't Jesus I lost faith in, it was my father, and those who didn't intervene on my behalf." I rested my head on Randy's shoulder and wept, feeling my own brokenness for the first time.

I whispered, "The world feels fatherless."

Randy held my hand tightly. "Perhaps, but it's not without love."

The lingering silence between us wove a deeper connection than any we'd experienced before. Somehow, my grieving was liberating, and I didn't regret what it took to break through my defenses. I knew we had everything of real importance with us. We had each other, our beloved dogs that were like family, our integrity and a new understanding of the power of our faith in Christ and what it meant to travel through dark, enigmatic times.

I then wondered whether parts of my own life had really been any different than I imagined an Arabian woman's might be. Had I avoided the anxiety and pain in my own life because it was overwhelming? Perhaps my appearance of strength had only been a cover for my emotional wounds. Perhaps it was my own trauma that I sensed when I saw veiled *Bedouin* women. Real courage, I decided, must be found by being honest with myself and grieving over the voids in my own life without dismissing myself. I must break the ineffective pattern of coping and the spells of worthlessness that I had internalized while younger. I did not want to pass them on to others.

Soon, the pilot announced our approach to the Athenian airport. We heard the clunk of the landing gear go down and lock into place. Randy and I picked up our carry-on baggage and prepared to deboard. I felt like a load had been lifted from my shoulders.

The night sky of Athens was just beginning to lighten. The buildings were still dark against the gray sky, and travelers wandered aimlessly around the terminal waiting for businesses and counters to open. I settled in a corner near the police guard and waited anxiously for Randy to exchange our money and make hotel reservations. He finally returned and we left the terminal, hoping to get settled quickly.

Taxi drivers refused to take us on account of our dogs, so we were forced to rent an old small car. Spending extra money for a rental was stressful, but the drivers had no idea what we had just been through. Driving toward the old part of Athens near the Acropolis, we got lost on the many winding streets. We were confused by the strange environment and Greek alphabet. I could hardly recall the Greek I'd studied while in seminary. It took us two hours to find the hotel, and when we arrived, the manager refused to register us when he saw how large our dogs were.

Disheartened, we decided to search for a place on foot. We parked the car, cracked open the windows and left the dogs inside. When we walked through an upscale shopping center, I paused in front of an elegant jewelry store. The satin covered shelves were laden with sparkling diamonds and glistening gold jewelry.

Randy moved closer and said, "I'm sorry I never bought you that beautiful sapphire bracelet you liked back in Saudi. I won't be able to do that now."

"It doesn't matter anymore. They don't define my worth. Those gems have no more value now than the gravel under my feet." I realized that luxury seduces us into a deep sleep and keeps us from seeing what's really important. In that way, consumerism is a thief that robs us of ourselves.

He smiled as we turned away from the store and walked on hand in hand.

While searching the city streets for hotel accommodations, we must have looked like lost, worn out tourists. A short Greek man approached us and offered to help us find a hotel. When Randy explained that we had two large dogs and little money, the man paused.

"I have a friend who runs a hotel. He might help you. Follow me."

We followed him down a narrow, winding side-street, where a number of towering hotels and small restaurants were located. He pushed open a door of a small hotel and entered the lobby. I looked through its front window and glanced around the simple, but neat place. "This hotel will work if they take dogs."

"I can hardly keep my eyes open, and I'm getting a headache. Do you still have our passports in a safe place?" he asked.

I pointed to the pack around my waist. "Everything we have is in here."

The little man returned smiling and said, "My friend says you can bring the dogs. Just leave them on the rooftop at night. It is nice and overlooks our beautiful city of Athena. The room is twelve dollars and breakfast is included."

Randy looked relieved and agreed to take it. The Greek smiled and turned around. He disappeared down the cobbled stone street that wound amongst the hotels and storefronts. He had been an answer to prayers not yet uttered.

We knew our cash would last longer now, and we'd have time to plan our next step. We traced our way back to the car, found the dogs sleeping and drove to the hotel. The dogs followed us up six flights of stairs to a small, clean room. Collapsing into bed, Randy and I put our arms around one another and fell into a deep sleep. For now, the small room was home.

We woke up later in the afternoon but continued to rest. By evening we decided to unwind with a glass of red wine and enjoy the view of the city from the hotel's rooftop. We sat on a deck swing and the dogs curled up at our feet. Randy put his arm around me. As the sun set behind the Parthenon on the hill of the Acropolis, we each raised a glass to toast the freedoms of the civilized world. Amongst the ancient ruins and modern buildings, the lights of Athens began to sparkle. Church bells rang freely in the distance and a shadow of a cross on a nearby Greek Orthodox Church crawled our way.

I set my glass down on a table next to the swing. "We are free to go to church now."

"I won't take that for granted anymore, and I want to buy one of those Greek Orthodox crosses for our home in California. That way we'll always remember we found a safe place in Greece."

"From America, Greece seemed so far away. But now I feel at home here," I added.

"This country laid the foundations of Western civilization. Plato, Socrates, Aristotle. I can see the similarities now: the architecture, the churches, men and women gazing romantically into one another's eyes, the dance halls loud and open. I see a sense of life and joy here."

"And women can drive!" I exclaimed.

"And you can skate again," he said, smiling.

"Since we're here, I want to visit Mars Hill where Paul preached near the Acropolis," I said. "Let's just make the best of it."

"Wasn't King Saud exiled to Athens when his brother Faisal deposed him and took over the crown?" asked Randy.

"That's right. The brothers said Saud was incompetent and a danger to the country. They never forgave him. He died here. And he was one of their own."

Two weeks later, we rented a farmhouse from a balding and robust butcher. His farm was located outside of Athens and near the coast of the Aegean Sea. He was happy to accommodate our dogs because his farm housed fifty hunting dogs. A man full of kindness, he provided us with logs for the fireplace, homemade wine and fresh sausages from his shop.

Once settled, we began our search for our next job and were delighted to find one in the city of Athens at an American International School. While working there, we received news from George and Lydia who were still in Saudi Arabia. They secretly forwarded a letter from Majid.

Dear Mr. and Mrs. Decker,

How are you? We all really miss you and no one believes what we've heard about what you guys did. We don't believe it. We know you were lied about. He's doing the same thing to our new teachers too.

I'm a lot taller now. I will always remember you and never forget you when I see or read or hear this poem by Frost:

Nothing Gold Can Stay

Nature's first green is gold
Her hardest hue to hold
Her early leaf's a flower
but only so an hour
Then leaf subsides to leaf
So Eden sank to grief
So dawn goes down to day
Nothing gold can stay.

My friend Ahmed asks about you. He doesn't believe that stuff either. He knows you didn't do anything wrong. We went to Egypt finally and saw the Pyramids but not the tomb of Tutankhamen.

Majid

I folded Majid's letter carefully and put it back in the envelope. Randy's eyes reddened. He wondered if I would work for them if they asked us.

"No," I said. "Our forgiveness is given freely, but trust has been completely broken. It would take a lifetime to earn back our trust. At least his letter gives me a sense of closure."

When the school year ended in Greece, I watched the American and international students check out and fly home to their families. Even though I was still frightened about returning to California, and didn't have a job to return to, our home was vacant, and our return plane tickets were only valid for another month. If we didn't return now, it would be extremely difficult to find the money to return anytime soon. Overcome with a strong desire to return, I decided to take the risk. Randy saw me off at the airport but remained in Greece for a couple of weeks with the dogs, to finish the job.

Ten hours later, my plane landed in New York. When I walked onto American soil, I was so overcome with emotion and appreciation for America and its hard won freedoms that I wanted to kiss the ground. However, I simply proceeded toward customs, fearing others would think I was crazy and would belittle my intense feelings.

The cheerful customs agent returned my passport. "Welcome back to America, Mrs. Decker. I see you've been gone quite some time."

"You have no idea how good it is to be back," I said, smiling.

"I've heard that before! Good luck to you now," he said with a nod.

I thanked him and tucked my passport back into my purse and headed for the next gate. Soon I boarded the plane bound for California.

Though it felt like the Fourth of July, it was eleven thirty p.m. on the third of July when I landed in Los Angeles. The familiar horizon filled with high rises and a grid of sparkling city lights was a welcomed scene. I took a shuttle bus home and paid the driver his tip while he unloaded my four worn suitcases. The tree-lined streets were smooth and missing the dust of the Saudi streets and the many potholes I'd dodged while driving in Greece.

I dragged my luggage across the street and stood reverently before my home. Everything was undisturbed, clean and in its place. The trees and flowerbeds were neatly trimmed. Small garden lights along the brick walk shone softly like opals and created silhouettes of the tall lampposts in the center of the yard. The neighborhood slept restfully.

Home, I thought, *a place of restoration*. It seemed an eternity had passed since I'd said good-bye to it. I hung my head with gratitude and whispered a prayer of thanks to God to be home. Knowing how easily it could have been lost, I knew I'd never take my home or way of life for granted again. I felt an added comfort, realizing that one day I would dwell in the house of the Lord forever, a home that would never be taken away.

Slowly, I walked toward the front door and fumbled for the key in my purse. I crossed the threshold and flicked on the light. The electricity was off, but I didn't care. I silently closed the door behind me and leaned against it. The garden lights shone through the open windows, and I could see the furnishings I had so carefully selected and arranged years before: the cherry bookcase, the college and seminary books carefully lining its shelves, the family pictures as well as the dining room hutch full of wedding gifts. All of the memories of our life together were safely in one place. I felt as if my home was welcoming my return and showing me a part of who I was and what was most important.

Leaving the luggage in the living room, I walked up the stairs in the darkness to wash. The water was cold, but it felt welcome on my dry and dirty skin. I searched in the shadows for our large bed. The firm mattress and warm comforter were things I'd grown unaccustomed to over the last year. I rested my head on the familiar pillow and slowly closed my eyes.

Randy would ship Aslan and Cheyenne home next week. He'd follow them a week later, and then we would all be home and could begin to heal. After their arrival, I'd plant flowers in my garden and wait for them to bloom; flowers that would be as beautiful as the pink cherry blossoms of China and the wild irises in the deserts of Arabia; flowers that would be so lovely they would cause me to forgive any winter its harshness and any desert its searing heat.

EPILOGUE

RANDAL AND KRISTIN returned to the United States in 1998. Kristin resumed her teaching career in public schools and now teaches U.S. History at the 8th grade level. Randal entered the financial services industry. He was later diagnosed and treated for cancer of the esophagus. After a year and a half of remission, the cancer returned to other abdominal organs. As of this writing he continues to battle this disease. The couple now resides comfortably in Texas with their two golden retrievers, Aslan and Angel. Cheyenne was diagnosed with lung cancer and passed away in July of 2006.

Several years after the Deckers left Saudi Arabia, the Arab News reported that Majid graduated from the Saudi public school with his proud father and grandfather looking on. Later, Prince Majid graduated from a Western university. International news reports confirmed that Prince Faisal suffered a heart attack and died in 2001. He was forty-four. The children are now adults and pursuing their royal duties. Though they answer to their paternal grandfather, Majid runs the family affairs in place of his father, and Samira plans to marry. The princess still resides in Riyadh but travels frequently.

The Phelps have retired with a comfortable income in the United States. They received special honor and remuneration from the royal family upon retiring. The Barkers still serve in international schools and are raising their son. The compound where Anna and Mohammed resided was one of several American compounds that were bombed by terrorists in Riyadh. Randal and Kristin saw the bombed apartment building in the news but do not know if Mohammed and Anna survived the attack. The whereabouts of Akbar and Seid are unknown. Rumors circulated that Akbar's parents had found him a suitable bride in India. Thousands of people from developing countries continue to struggle and suffer in the land of Saudi Arabia.

"No one will tell King Fahad that there are poor people in the Kingdom," Majid explained one day in class.
"Why not?" I asked.

"Because he would get upset."
It is not proper for one to be the bearer of bad news.

KRISTIN

THE COMPOUND

THE COMPOUND

ASLAN

CHEYENNE

INSIDE THE VILLA

READY FOR A WEDDING

INSIDE THE MALL

CAMEL RIDE

RANDY AT DIRIYAH

SHIFTING SANDS

RANDY AND KRISTIN

IN THE CLASSROOM

GLOSSARY

Abaya – Women's cloak-like covering that is worn in public at all times

Allah- Arabic for God, derivative of Elohim, Hebrew for God

Bahrain – The island nation situated in the Persian, or Arabian, Gulf

Bin/Bint - Son of, or daughter of

Caliph – Successor to Mohammed

Dar-al-Harb – An abode of conflict in which unbelievers dwell

Dar-es-Salam – An abode of peace in which followers of Mohammed dwell

Dhimmi – Christians and Jews living in an Islamic culture with second-class status before law

Diriyah – The old city of Riyadh in the midst of a *wadi*

Fatwa – Religious ruling issued by an *Imam*

Ghutra – Head scarf worn by men in Arabia

Hajj – Pilgrimage to Mecca required of all Muslims at least once in a lifetime

Halas – Finished, done

Hanbali School – School of thought that follows the teachings of tenth century leader Mohamed Al-Hanbal

Ibn – Son of

Igaal – Headband that holds a headscarf in place, often a black cord

Ikhwan – Zealous religious fighters originally loyal to King Abdul-Aziz

Imam – Living heir of Mohammed

Iman – Seed or grain of faith that grants one passage into Paradise

Jinn – Created being similar to angels that sit upon one's shoulders

Majlis – Meeting place that is established by a leading sheik for the purpose of listening to the needs of tribal leaders

Manama, Bahrain – Capital city of Bahrain, located in the Persian Gulf

Mismaak – The fortress in Riyadh captured by Abdul Aziz in 1902

Muezzin – Individual who cries out the call to prayer over loudspeakers

Mullah – Religious leader or cleric

Mutawwa (ain) – Morality police who patrol the city

Nadj – Region of Central Arabia

Nasiriyah – Palace district in Riyadh where wealthy Saudis and royal family members reside

Qur'an – The text received by the prophet Mohammed and delivered by the angel Gabriel

Ramadan – Month of fasting set aside to honor the time Mohammed received the revelations in the *Qur'an*

Riyal – Saudi Arabian currency unit

Sabah 'al Hare – Greeting for "Good Morning"

Sabah 'al Noor – Greeting for "Good Evening"

Salat – Ritual prayer observed at appointed times each day, a pillar of Islam

Shahada – Confession of faith that honors God as one and Mohammed as his prophet

Sharia – Divine-inspired law that governs daily life of Muslims

Sheik – Teacher of Islam

Shia – Minority sect of Islam that traces Mohammed's successor through the Caliph Abu Baker

Souk – Open market for local merchants

Sufism – Mystical sect of Islam considered corrupt by Wahabbi fundamentalists

Sunni – Majority sect of Islam that traces Mohammed's successor through Mohammed's son-in-law

Suras – Chapter divisions of the *Qur'an*

Thobe – The long white robe frequently worn by Arabian men

Wadi – Settlement near an oasis or watering hole

Wahabbi – Religious sect in Saudi Arabia revived under Mohammed Al-Wahab during the time of Mohammed Al-Saud

Zakat – Charity given to the poor, one of the pillars of Islam

Zuhr – The noon prayer time

ENDNOTES BY CHAPTER

CHAPTER 2 RESOURCES USED:

1. Lacey, Robert, <u>The Kingdom</u>, pg. 30
2. Lacey, Robert, <u>The Kingdom</u>, pg. 287
3. Lacey, Robert, <u>The Kingdom</u>, pg. 143
4. Mackey, Sandra, <u>The Saudis</u>, pg. 197
5. Mackey, Sandra, <u>The Saudis</u>, pg. 130

CHAPTER 3

1. Lacey, Robert, <u>The Kingdom</u>, pg. 146
2. Bard, <u>The Middle East Conflict</u>, pg. 66
3. Jurgensmeyer, Mark, <u>Terror in the Mind of God</u>, pg. 81
4. Bard, <u>The Middle East Conflict</u>, pg. 54
5. Mackey, Sandra, <u>The Saudis</u>, pgs. 68, 69
6. Goodwin, Jan, <u>The Price of Honor</u>, pg. 212
7. Mackey, Sandra, <u>The Saudis</u>, pg. 201

CHAPTER 4

1. Bin Laden, Carmen, <u>Inside the Kingdom</u>, pg. 4
2. Bin Laden, Carmen, <u>Inside the Kingdom</u>, pg. 5
3. PBS/Frontline, *House of Saud*, 2003
4. Goodwin, Jan, <u>The Price of Honor</u>, pg. 211
5. Jurgensmeyer, Mark, <u>Terror in the Mind of God</u>, pg. 69
6. Brown, Colin, <u>Philosophy and the Christian Faith</u>, pg. 45
7. Schaeffer, Francis, <u>How then Should We Live</u>, pg. 43
8. PBS/Frontline, *House of Saud*, 2003
9. Schaeffer, Francis, <u>How then Should We Live</u>, pg.130

CHAPTER 5
1. Lacey, Robert, <u>The Kingdom,</u> pg. 147
2. PBS/Frontline, *The House of Saud*, 2003
3. Lacey, Robert, <u>The Kingdom,</u> pg.174
4. Lacey, Robert, <u>The Kingdom,</u> pg. 364

CHAPTER 6

1. Mackey, Sandra, <u>The Saudis,</u> pg. 163
2. Lacey, Robert, <u>The Kingdom,</u> pgs. 367, 368
3. PBS/Frontline, *The House of Saud,* 2003

CHAPTER 9
1. Lacey, Robert, <u>The Kingdom,</u> pg. 370
2. Mackey, Sandra, <u>The Saudis,</u> pg. 201
3. Thompson, Ionis, <u>Desert Treks around Riyadh,</u> pg. 40
4. Bard, <u>Middle East Conflict,</u> pg. 66
5. Sancton & McCleod, BBC, *Death of a Princess*

CHAPTER 10

1. Moore, Thomas, <u>Job,</u> pg. xxi

CHAPTER 11

1. Brown, Colin, <u>Philosophy,</u> pg. 44

CHAPTER 12

1. Machiavelli, <u>The Prince</u>

CHAPTER 15

1. Bard, <u>The Middle East Conflict,</u> pg. 61
2. Bard, <u>The Middle East Conflict,</u> pg. 62
3. Bard, <u>The Middle East Conflict,</u> pg. 66

BIBLIOGRAPHY

Ahmed, Akbar	Discovering Islam, Routledge & Kegan Paul Ltd., London, 1988
Aquinas, Thomas	Summa Theologiae, Vol. 1, Image Books, NY, 1969
Alexander, Lloyd	The Remarkable Journey of Prince Jen, Doubleday, NY, 1991
Bard, Mitchell	The Middle East Conflict, MacMillan, IN, 1999
Beyer, Lisa	"Inside the Kingdom," Time Magazine, 9-15-03
Bin Laden, Carmen	Inside the Kingdom, Warner Books, NY, 2004
Brown, Collin	Philosophy and the Christian Faith, Inter Varsity Press, Ill, 1968
Brooks, Geraldine	Nine Parts of Desire, Anchor Books, NY, 1995
Caner Ergun Mehmet	Voices Behind the Veil, Kregel Publications, Grand Rapids, MI, 03
Doumato, Eleanor	Getting God's Ear, Columbia University Press, NY, 2000
Goodwin, Jan	Price of Honor, Little, Brown & Co., NY, 1994
Juergensmeyer, Mark	Terror in the Mind of God, U of CA Press, 2000
Keller, Phillip	A Shepherd Looks at Psalm 23, Zondervan, Grand Rapids, MI, 1970
Lacey, Robert	The Kingdom, Harcourt- Brace-Jovanovich, London, 1981
Lewis, Bernard	What Went Wrong? Perennial-Harper Collins, NY, 2002
Luther, Dr. Martin	Luther, Lectures on Romans, the Westminster Press, PA, 1959
Luther, Dr. Martin	Bondage of the Will, Fleming H. Revell, 1957
McDowell, Josh	A Ready Defense, Thomas Nelson, Nashville, TN, 1993
Machiavelli, Niccolo	The Prince, Bantam Books, NY, translated 1966

Mackey, Sandra	The Saudis, W.W. Norton & Co., NY, 2002 update
Moor, Thomas	The Book of Job, Riverhead Books, NY, 1998
Nafisi, Azar	Reading Lolita in Tehran, Random House, NY, 2003
Oufkir, Malika	Stolen Lives, Hyperion, NY, 1999
Fitoussi, Michele	
Posner, Gerald	Why America Slept, Random House, NY, 2003
PBS	*House of Saud,* Frontline, 2003
Queen Noor,	Leap of Faith, Miramax Books, NY, 2003
Sasson, Jean	Princess, Avon Books, NY, 1992
Sasson, Jean	Princess Sultana's Circle, Windsor-Brooke Books, NY, 2000
Schaeffer, Francis	Escape from Reason, Inter Varsity Press, Illinois, 1968
Schaeffer, Francis	How then Should We Live? Crossway Books, Wheaton, Ill., 1976
Tarnas, Richard,	The Passion of the Western Mind, Ballantine Books, NY, 1991
Thompson, Ionis	Desert Treks from Riyadh, Stacey International, London, 1994
Viviano, Frank	"Saudi Arabia on the Edge," National Geographic, Oct., 2003
Von Loewenich	Luther's Theology of the Cross, Augsburg, Minneapolis, MN, 1982

LaVergne, TN USA
17 November 2009
164327LV00003B/10/A